Desperate Voyage

*Donald Crowhurst, The London Sunday
Times Golden Globe Race,
and the Tragedy of Teignmouth Electron*

Edward Renehan

*To Alan
with all good wishes
Edward Renehan*

2016

NEW STREET COMMUNICATIONS, LLC
Wickford, Rhode Island

Library of Congress Control Number: 2016911799

Paperback published August 2016 by
NEW STREET COMMUNICATIONS, LLC
Wickford, Rhode Island

Kindle Edition Published July 2016
Audio Edition Published September 2016

newstreetcommunications.com

Dedicated to my grandson
CONNOR WILLIAM SHARP
with the hope that he will always
choose his races wisely,
run them fairly,
and find his own best self
in the process.

Full fathom five thy father lies;
Of his bones are coral made;
Those are pearls that were his eyes;
Nothing of him that doth fade,
But doth suffer a sea-change
Into something rich and strange.
Sea-nymphs hourly ring his knell:
Ding-dong.
Hark! now I hear them — Ding-dong, bell.

- William Shakespeare, *The Tempest* -

Table of Contents

Teignmouth Electron *as she looks today on Cayman Brac.*
Photos: Eric Loss. All rights reserved. Used by permission.

Introduction

Close to the shore on lonely Cayman Brac – 90 miles (145 km) northeast of Grand Cayman and five and a half miles (9 km) east of Little Cayman – a savaged hull and two smaller rotted floats protrude from a cluster of beach pines. The boat – once a sharp-looking trimaran – is as broken as a vessel can be, and as broken as an ill-founded pipe dream inevitably becomes. Souvenir hunters have carved out places on the bow where the boat's name, *Teignmouth Electron*, once appeared. At the stern a visitor has scrawled the words "dream Boat" [sic]. This is all that's left of Donald Crowhurst's ill-fated voyage of 1968/69 – this along with a shattered family, and a story. More accurately: a cautionary tale about self-deceit, misguided ambition, and – on the part of some, though not Crowhurst – hubris.

Many thousands of miles away, in a cottage near Seaton – less than an hour from the Devon coastal town of Teignmouth from which Donald Crowhurst set out on the last day of October, 1968 – Crowhurst's elderly widow Clare sits and contemplates the past. "For years I thought [Donald] could have survived," she has told BBC journalist Chris Eakin. "Now, I think he definitely died at that time. But how he died? I find it impossible, knowing the person, to believe that he committed suicide. I still find that impossible to believe. … I think of him every single day … . It has been a disaster. I think it has been a disaster for the children even more, their father being missing which is, God knows, enough, but it has shaped their lives, without doubt."

The *London Sunday Times* Golden Globe Race of 1968 and 1969 remains one of the truly great sea-going epochs of modern times. The Golden Globe Trophy was to go to the first entrant who completed a *solo non-stop round-the-world voyage* under sail via the three great capes of the Southern Ocean (South Africa's Cape of Good Hope, Australia's Cape Leeuwin, and Chile's Cape Horn) – a feat never before accomplished. Since participants would be leaving from different ports within a time-window of several months, a second prize of £5,000 would go to the sailor recognized for the *fastest* completion of the same voyage, this calculated on a lapsed-time basis. Entrants were permitted to leave any port of their choice (that is, any port above 40° N) at any time between 1st June and 31st October 1968. (Departure much later than 31st October would have put an entrant in the perilous Southern Ocean – the notorious "Roaring Forties" – at the start of the Southern winter, when genuinely treacherous waters became even more-so.) To qualify for the lapsed-time award, entrants had to depart from and arrive at a port in Britain.

The eventual winner of both the Golden Globe and the lapsed-time race, Robin Knox-Johnston, was a seasoned 28-year-old sailor and merchant officer who sailed a 32-foot Bermudan ketch. The other major entrants – Frenchmen Bernard Moitessier and Loïck Fougeron, Italian Alex Carozzo (the so-called "Chichester of Italy"), and Brits Bill Leslie King,

John Ridgway, Chay Blyth, Nigel Tetley, and Donald Crowhurst – ran the gamut of personalities, experience, and sailing craft.

Of all these, Donald Crowhurst was the least likely and, ultimately, the most tragic.

In 1970, not long after Donald Crowhurst's death, Nicholas Tomalin and Ron Hall assembled a masterful narrative entitled *The Strange Last Voyage of Donald Crowhurst*, this published in England by Hoddard & Stoughton. Today the book remains a true classic of maritime literature. However, there is new information. Documentaries produced and interviews published in the years after *The Strange Last Voyage of Donald Crowhurst* allow for enhanced insights with regard to several key aspects of the story. I endeavor to make maximum use of all these materials. As well, concerns that Tomalin and Hall quite rightly had regarding libel have gone away with the deaths of two key players whose roles in Crowhurst's misadventure were at times less than honorable: businessman Stanley Best and publicist Rodney Hallworth. Thus I hope to shed more light on the story than could be done in 1970.

Edward Renehan
Wickford, RI
14 July 2016

Chapter One: Forerunners

The first documented solo circumnavigation of the globe was, of course, that of native Nova Scotian Joshua Slocum. Slocum's voyage – transacted aboard the *Spray*, a rebuilt 36' 9" (11.2 m) gaff-rigged oyster sloop – took place from 24th April 1895 to 27th June 1898, departing from Boston and arriving at Newport, RI. Slocum made many stops along the way to rest himself and refit his vessel, and used the Strait of Magellan rather than braving Cape Horn.

Somewhat astonishingly, Slocum – by his own account in his 1899 book *Saling Alone Around the World* – relied primarily on pure traditional dead reckoning for calculating longitude, using a simple clock rather than the standard chronometer. And he calculated latitude using noon-sun sights. (During one extended passage he verified his longitude calculations by shooting a lunar observation – but he did this only once throughout his entire circumnavigation.)

Importantly, Slocum's vessel seems to have been especially well-configured for single-handed sailing. Given an optimal length-of-sail plan in relation to the hull, and an extended keel, the sloop seemed almost made to accommodate self-steering. Slocum was easily able to balance the *Spray* on a steady course in any wind simply by lashing the helm and adjusting or reefing sails as necessary. According to his book, Slocum sailed a full 2000 miles (3,200 km) west across the Pacific without touching the helm.

Slocum's *Sailing Alone Around the World* became a bestseller both in the United States and Europe. Royalties and fees for public appearances – including bringing his *Spray* up the Hudson and through the Erie Canal to Buffalo's Pan American Exhibition during the summer of 1901 – brought him a measure of financial security. However, in his last years both his finances and his mental stability failed. He effectively abandoned his wife and family, settling them on a small farm at West Tisbury on Martha's Vineyard, and lived alone aboard the increasingly rundown *Spray*, which he sailed from port to port along the American east coast, giving talks and selling books when he could. Slocum and the *Spray* were lost at sea in November or December of 1909 during a voyage from New England to the West Indies, where Slocum had intended to winter.

The second man to solo circumnavigate the world was American Harry Pidgeon.

A photographer by trade, the 47-year-old Iowa native built his 34-foot yawl *Islander* alone, by hand, over the years 1917 and 1918, at a cost of $1000. He constructed the vessel in the port of Los Angeles on beach-front land where he held nothing more than squatter's rights.

Pidgeon crafted the *Islander* using $2 "build-it-yourself" plans from *Rudder Magazine*. Specifically, he used Frederick William Goeller, Jr.'s design called *Seagoer* – this principally an enlarged version of Thomas Fleming Day's very popular *Sea Bird*. (Pidgeon built his vessel from Oak, Oregon Pine, and Douglas Fir. Length overall was 34 feet [10.36 m], beam: 10' feet 9 inches [3.32 m], draft: 5 feet [1.524 m], weight: 19 tons.)

Pidgeon had up to this time been nothing but a weekend coastal sailor. His sea-trials for the *Islander* consisted of several short sails to Catalina Island and back, these followed by a more extensive round-trip voyage to Hawaii. In November of 1921 – *at age 52* – he commenced a four-year solo circum-navigation. Pidgeon set out for the Marquesas Islands, then proceeded to Samoa, Fiji, New Hebrides, New Guinea, the Torres Strait, Christmas Island, the Cocos Islands, Mauritius, Cape Town, St. Helena, Ascension Island, Trinidad, Cris-tobal, and the Panama Canal, arriving back at Los Angeles in October 1925.

Throughout the trip, Pidgeon navigated mostly by simple sun-sights. Like Slocum before him, Pidgeon avoided the treacherous Cape Horn. Just as Slocum had bypassed Cape Horn via the Strait of Magellan, Pidgeon avoided Cape Horn via the Panama Canal. However, both men traversed similar (though slightly less severe) seas to those found at South America's Cape Horn when they rounded South Africa's Cape of Good Hope and Australia's Cape Leeuwin – true tests for any solo sailor. Pidgeon repeated his voyage using the same vessel during the years 1932 through 37.

Both Slocum and Pidgeon had good reason to avoid Cape Horn, the most treacherous spot in the entire Southern Ocean. As Peter Nichols notes in his masterful *A Voyage for Madmen*:

> *At 57 degrees south, Cape Horn forced ships to their farthest, coldest, stormiest south … . Here, Southern Ocean winds and waters are funneled through a relatively narrow gap, Drake Strait, the 600-mile-wide sea passage between Cape Horn and the Antarctic peninsula. … williwaws of hurricane-force winds scream down off the Andean glaciers; wind, towering waves, and ferocious currents collide, turning Cape Horn waters into a maelstrom. [It has become known] as "the graveyard of the sea."*

Pidgeon recounted his initial circumnavigation in *Around the World Single-Handed*, published 1933. The book began as an extensively illustrated article published in the February 1928 *National Geographic*, and grew from there. In 1926 Pidgeon received the coveted Blue Water Medal from the Cruising Club of America in recognition of "outstanding seafaring expertise." Pidgeon continued with extensive sailing for the rest of his life and died of pneumonia on 11th April 1954 in San Pedro, California, aged 85.

More than a dozen mariners successfully circum-navigated solo up to 1966, a few using the Panama Canal, one using the Suez Canal, and several the Strait of Magellan. But many braved the dangerous "Roaring Forties" of the Southern Ocean to wrestle all three capes. All, meanwhile, made numerous stops.

During 1966 and '67, Britain's Francis Chichester dealt with all three capes and made history by logging a solo voyage with only one stop (107 days at Sydney, Australia) for rest and refit, a voyage which was also the fastest circumnavigation to date at nine months and one day. Born in 1901, Chichester was 65 when he set out on his voyage. He had previously been a record-making aviator, having made the first solo flight across the Tasman Sea from east to west (New Zealand to Australia). After World War II, he founded a successful map publishing and marketing company which later branched out into tourist guidebooks, and had a shop in London.

In 1958, after being diagnosed with terminal lung cancer (which subsequently went into remission for a number of years), the indomitable 57-year-old took up yachting for the first time. A mere two years later, he won the first transatlantic single-handed race founded that year by Lieutenant Colonel "Blondie Hasler," inventor of self-steering gear still popular among yachtsmen. Chichester attempted the same race in '64, coming in as a runner-up.

Chichester transacted his circumnavigation in *Gipsy Moth IV*: a 53 foot (16 m) yawl specially designed for the voyage by Angus Primrose and John Illingworth, and built by Camper & Nicholson of Gosport, South Hampshire. Chichester financed part of the construction himself, but for the majority of the budget relied on his cousin, Lord Dulverton. Despite the fact that *Gipsy Moth IV* had been commissioned and carefully architected with Chichester's voyage in mind, Chichester in retrospect had many complaints to make about the vessel. When asked about its disposition, he responded: "Now that I have finished, I don't know what will become of *Gipsy Moth IV*. I only own the stern while my cousin owns two thirds. My part, I would sell any day. It would be better if about a third were sawn off. The boat was too big for me. *Gipsy Moth IV* has no sentimental value for me at all. She is cantankerous and difficult and needs a crew of three – a man to navigate, an elephant to move the tiller, and a 3'6" (1.1 m) chimpanzee with arms 8' (2.4 m) long to get about below and work some of the gear."

By the time Chichester sailed into Plymouth Hoe at the conclusion of his circumnavigation on 28th May 1967, he had – despite his vessel's shortcomings – logged not only the fastest circumnavigation by any small vessel, but also the longest non-stop passage (15,000 miles – 24,140 km). He twice made records for a single-hander's week's run, and he created a new record for single-handed speed when he sailed 1,400 miles (2,253 km) in the scope of a mere 8 days. All of this he chronicled in his 1967 book *Gipsy Moth Circles the World*. Upon his return, Chichester was knighted by Queen Elizabeth. He also became the first non-Royal to get his face on a postage stamp during his lifetime. (In 1970, sailing *Gipsy Moth V*, the 69-year-old would endeavor to sail 4,000 miles [6437.38 km] in twenty days, but missed the mark by one day. He died of his cancer in 1972.) [1]

----

1   Note: Alec Rose repeated Chichester's achievement, departing 16th July 1967 and arriving back in Southsea, England on 4th July 1968, with stops in Australia and New Zealand. Like Chichester, Rose received a knighthood.

The London *Sunday Times* and *Guardian* newspapers purchased shared rights for reporting the first half of Chichester's adventure of 1966 and 1967. Halfway through, the cash-strapped *Guardian* dropped out, but the *Sunday Times* continued its sponsorship and soon reaped large rewards in headlines and sales as interest in Chichester (at first tepid) rose slowly and unpredictably to a fever pitch. Thereafter, the newspaper became deeply interested in sponsoring further daring nautical adventures – preferably of the record-breaking variety.

Chapter Two: Origins Of The Race

In the wake of Chichester's conquest, yachtsmen wishing to make a mark in the annals of circumnavigation realized there remained only one more great mountain to climb: a solo *non-stop* round-the-world voyage with no shortcuts round the capes of the Southern Ocean. (Chichester himself called this challenge "The Everest of the Sea.") It was not long before several likely contenders – and several unlikely contenders – began to make plans.

One of the first men to begin serious work turned out, in the end, to be the first and only man to finish what became the *Sunday Times* Golden Globe Race. William Robert Patrick ("Robin") Knox-Johnston had been born in London in 1939, the eldest of four brothers. He entered the Merchant Navy at

18, becoming a Deck Officer on vessels of the British India Steam Navigation Company. Knox-Johnston married in 1962 and became the father of a daughter, Sara, in 1963, while the family was living in Bombay. He earned his Master's Certificate in 1965.

Knox-Johnston commissioned the building of his William Atkins designed, 32 foot (9.8 m) ketch *Suhaili* in India during 1963. He sailed her home to England in 1965 – a voyage during which she performed well. Knox-Johnston initially contemplated the building of a larger vessel for his solo round-the-world attempt, but in the end he settled on *Suhaili* as the vessel he'd use. Bluff, physically strong, and eminently competent, Knox-Johnston seemed not only to have the skills required for the task, but also the psychology: emotionally balanced and enormously self-confident.

The next strongest contender was Frenchman Bernard Moitessier. Born in 1925 and raised for the most part in Vietnam during that nation's time as a French colonial outpost, Moitessier combined a mercurial personality with a deeply-philosophical love for the sea. He cared little for worldly things or, for that matter, human society, which he saw as being materialistic, plastic, and trivial. As he would write: "I have no desire to return to Europe with all its false gods. They eat your liver out and suck your marrow and brutalize you. I am going where you can tie up a boat where you want and the sun is free, and so is the air you breathe and the sea where you swim and you can roast yourself on a coral reef."

With his wife Françoise, he'd spent more than two years sailing from France to Casablanca, thence to the Canaries,

Trinidade, the Galapagos Islands (via the Panama Canal), and Tahiti, spending extended periods at each destination. All the while, the couple left their three children in the hands of European boarding schools. Departing Tahiti for their return voyage to France, the couple, took the most direct but also most treacherous route, rounding Cape Horn. By the time they reached home at Easter of 1966 they'd (inadvertantly) accomplished the longest nonstop yacht voyage up to that date, traveling 14,216 nautical miles (22,878 km) over the course of 126 days. Their vessel – a steel-hulled 39-foot (11.8 m) ketch specially commissioned by Moitessier – was named *Joshua*, after Joshua Slocum. As Moitessier wrote in his 1967 book *Cap Horn à la Voile*, the vessel was "solid, simple, sure – and fast on all points of sailing."

Additional early contenders included John Ridgway (born 1938), a captain in the Special Air Service who was not a yachtsman but had gained notoriety when in 1966, with Sergeant Charles ("Chay") Blyth, he'd rowed across the Atlantic. Viewing the contemplated voyage as essentially an experiment in pure endurance, he planned to set out in a production line cruising sloop, *English Rose IV* – a vessel even smaller than Knox-Johnston's ketch, at a mere 30 feet (9.14 m), and entirely unsuitable (yachting pundits shouted) for the Southern Ocean. (Another contender, an Australian dentist and yachtsman well-known as "Tahiti Bill" Howell, also announced plans at about this time, but later dropped out.)

Finally, Bill Leslie King brought equally respectable credentials as those possessed by Knox-Johnston and Moitessier. A retired Royal Navy submarine commander, King (just two years shy of age 60 in 1968) was an experienced sailor who commissioned Blondie Hasler and Angus Primrose to create a vessel specially fitted for the voyage. Hasler designed the rig, and Primrose the hull. The improbable result – *Galway Blazer II* – wound up being a 42-foot (12.80 m) submarine-shaped, cold-molded plywood schooner sporting a flush "turtle back" deck and two junk-rigged masts, all specially designed to endure the constant storms of the Roaring Forties. King recruited the *Daily* and *Sunday Express* as newspaper sponsors.

Although others would soon start on similar plans, these four men – Knox-Johnston, Moitessier, Ridgway, and King – constituted the first wave of contenders with firm ambitions as of January 1968, well before the announcement of the race.

Robin Knox-Johnston made the shrewd move of hiring a prominent London literary agent, George Greenfield, to pre-sell a book about his voyage and to also recruit newspaper sponsorship. It was after Greenfield approached *Sunday Times* editor Harold Evans about newspaper sponsorship that the idea for what became the *Sunday Times* Golden Globe race began to evolve. In the end, it was Evans, working in conjunction with *Sunday Times* reporter Jonathan Sayle, who drafted the rules previously described: the parallel lapsed-time and first-round races, with the first carrying a £5,000 prize and the second the Golden Globe trophy.

There would be no formal entry process. Any sailor departing from any port north of 40° N at any time between 1st June and 31st October 1968, and who had his departure time and location formally documented by a national magazine or newspaper, would automatically be "enrolled" in the competition. (As noted previously, one further requirement was that, in order to win the lapsed-time race, one's arrival and departure had to be a port in Britain.)

The *Times* announced their race on 17th March. At the same time, they announced a panel of judges under the chairmanship of Chichester. Additional members included Dennis Hamilton (Chief Executive and Editor-in-Chief of Times Newspapers), Michael Richey (Executive Secretary of the Institute of Navigation), M. Alain Gliksman (noted French yachtsman and editor of *Neptune Nautisme*), and initially Blondie Hasler, who soon resigned due to his fear he was too closely associated with Bill Leslie King and *Galway Blazer II.*

Four other primary contenders soon materialized.

42-year-old Frenchman Loïck Fougeron was a seasoned yachtsman and close friend of Moitessier. Fougeron planned to embark upon *Captain Browne*, a 31 foot (9.5 m) steel cutter designed by Louis Van de Wiele. Italian Alex Carozzo likewise announced his intentions, and commissioned the building of a 66-foot (20.11 m) ketch, *Gancia Americano*, at Cowes. At the same time, John Ridgway's rowing companion, 28-year-old Scotsman Chay Blyth, entered with a vessel (a 30-foot [9.144 m] bilge-keeler named *Dytiscus III*) which was a virtual clone of that to be sailed by his friend Ridgway: two neophytes setting off with inadequate equipment, both of whom would perform respectably considering their inexperience and their production-line vessels. (In fact Blyth, a quick study, was in 1971 to become the first man to solo circumnavigate the world travelling from from east to west.) These men would eventually be joined by retired naval officer Nigel Tetley. More on him later.

Finally, there was Somerset businessman Donald Crowhurst – a figure nearly as unknown in yachting circles as were Ridgway and Blyth, and a man who seemed a conundrum in more ways than one.

Chapter Three: Enter Donald Crowhurst

The father of four, Donald Crowhurst owned a failing electronics concern based in the West Country at Bridgwater, Somerset. He'd been born in India in 1932, the son of second-generation colonials. His mother taught school. His father worked as a superintendant on the North Western India Railway. The father drank, and came across as severe and remote even when sober. The mother suffered recurrent fits of depression.

After Donald turned ten, the family relocated to Multan, Pakistan, where the father sunk his life savings into a sports-goods factory in partnership with a Pakistani native. When Donald reached age 14, his parents sent him back to England and enrolled him in Loughborough College. The parents returned to England one year later. With Pakistan roiling amid the chaos of partition, Mr. Crowhurst left the factory under the management of his partner. The Pakistan business soon failed, and the elder Crowhurst wound up having to take a low-paying job as a porter at a jam factory in Reading: a dramatic comedown for the once-prominent railway officer. He fell dead of a coronary in March of 1948.

Soon after, Donald passed the London University School Certificate exam and then attended the Royal Aircraft Establishment Technical College at Farnborough, focusing on electrical engineering. He spent several years in the Royal Air Force as a commissioned flyer. When not on duty, he pursued young manhood quite vigorously: many friends, much drink, numerous fast cars, and any woman he could catch. In short, he was in these respects the most typical of male individuals for his age, time, and place.

Things sometimes got a bit too wild. According to one source, when he left the RAF it was at his commander's request, after driving a motorcycle through a barracks. According to another, his sudden retirement occurred after a day when he decided to go racing cars at Brands Hatch rather than show up for an important – and mandatory – parade. Unphased, Crowhurst promptly got himself a commission in the army and began, through a military program, to seriously study electronic control equipment, becoming a member of the Royal Electrical and Mechanical Engineers. He received a discharge from the army in 1956, at age 24, after an incident involving a stolen car, at which point he tried but failed to pass the qualifying exams for Peterhouse, Cambridge. Though frustrated in his academic plans, he was nevertheless able, with his technical training, to get a minor research and development job in the laboratories at Reading University.

Clare O'Leary, whom Crowhurst met and married in 1957, had been raised on a farm in Killarney, Ireland. Irish Catholic on her father's side and Anglo-Irish Protestant on her mother's, she could claim relation on her mother's side to the prominent Talbot family. Their first son, James, arrived in 1958. Three more were to come: two boys, Simon and Roger, and a girl, Rachel, the youngest.

Rarely satisfied with the *status quo* – whatever it might be at any given moment – Crowhurst moved from job to job with some rapidity. For a time he worked for Mullard Limited as a salesman on the road, demonstrating their various semi-conductors and other electronic devices to potential purchasers. Then, after several more positions, he gained a position as Chief Design Engineer with an electronics firm in Bridgwater.

With his habit of questioning authority, he was by no means the ideal corporate man. His aim had long been to start and manage his own firm, free from the agendas of nagging superiors whom, in his view, were generally not his intellectual equals. Thus in the early 1960s he launched Electron Utilisation, marketing a device the idea for which had emerged from his newly-adopted hobby of weekend sailing in the Bristol Channel.

Electron Utilisation focused on what Crowhurst called the *Navicator*: a very simple radio-direction-finding device (RDF) which allowed mariners to take bearings using marine and aviation radio beacons. There were, at the time, many similar devices on the market, although the Navicator's unique pistol like shape, with a compass built in, made it easier to use than most.

Crowhurst loved tinkering with gadgets, trying to come up with patentable inventions, doing experiments, and solving technical problems with a boffin-like fascination. He could become immersed in his little workshop for many hours, happily separated from the cares of the household and unaware of anything save fuses and circuits. He also loved numbers – especially complex, abstract numbers. He eschewed the vagaries of spirituality in favor of provable, computational exactness and certitude.

Looking back on other aspects of his character as described by peers and friends, one senses that Crowhurst might well have been what we would today call a manic depressive: bipolar. From this distance, what we know of his personality certainly sounds bipolar. He cherished a series of great exuberances and grand schemes until, one by one, they came to nothing – leaving him adrift in profound doldrums until he moved on to his next fascination. When elevated, he inevitably over-reached, such as when he ran a failed campaign for Liberal councillor in the Bridgwater Central Ward while at the same time endeavoring to keep a struggling business afloat. He as well had a pronounced tendency – common in manics – toward grandiosity. He considered himself smarter than *most* people when in fact he was simply smarter than *many* people. Nevertheless, he acted the part, and believed he could always make impossible situations turn out right: until they didn't.

A Bridgwater friend, Peter Beard, would eventually comment: "The thing about Donald was that he thought himself God. Everything in his life revolved about his belief in himself, and he was always so quick and clever he could make others believe in him too. … But he wasn't God, and that's why all his troubles were his own fault." A failed RAF career, a failed army career, a failed attempt to qualify for Cambridge, brief and troubled tenures at a succession of firms – none of these things phased Crowhurst, or shook his over-arching belief in his superiority or, indeed, the inevitability of his eventual rise. Grand ambitions half achieved due to poor execution and then, one after another, abandoned – this, in the final analysis, was his pattern.

Electron Utilisation seems to have been a prime example of Crowhurst's penchant for over-reach. Even before he had secure marketing arrangements in hand and retailers signed up, he convinced his mother to sell her house in order to finance the firm. Then he leased factory-space, hired several employees, and set about production at a level that more than met the soft demand for Navicators – stockpiling a large back-inventory. At the same time, he bought a fine house – *Woodlands* – for himself and his family, as well as a Jaguar and a 20-foot sloop: all the accoutrements of a successful entre-preneur.

Although the Navicator device eventually garnered a small amount of popularity, revenue from sales never quite covered the overhead of the firm, let alone the overhead involved in supporting his family on an overly-grand, somewhat heroic scale. After the cash from the sale of Crowhurst's mother's house ran out, he received a reprieve from immediate ruin with an option payment from Cambridge-based Pye Radio, this towards acquisition of his firm. The payment helped cover his expenses for a bit longer. However, the Pye Radio acquisition never went forward, as Pye itself was in desperate financial shape following the British Trade Secretary's 1966 veto of its acquisition by Phillips.

Within a year, Crowhurst's problems had been compounded by the very slim margin which existed between his manufacturing cost and competitively-dictated retail pricing. To make ends meet, he closed his commercial space, moved manufacture into the stable at his home, and whittled his staff down to just one part-time helper. In early 1967, after numerous banks turned him down, he borrowed £1000 from Stanley Best – a wealthy dealer in caravans (motorhomes) from nearby Taunton – to help keep the firm alive.

Such was Crowhurst's situation on the day Chichester sailed into Plymouth Hoe to great honors, acclaim, and – as Donald Crowhurst quickly took note – the expectation of tremendous personal profit from his new celebrity in the way of a book deal, speaking fees, and attention to his small guide and map concern. The idea to repeat Chichester's feat beckoned. To Crowhurst, given his strained financial state and penchant for magical thinking, the thought of a romantic, grand gesture with which to redeem himself proved not only enticing, but irresistible: not just a solution, but an heroic one, and an escape. Whether or not the idea represented anything

realistic apparently did not enter into Crowhurst's calculations.

Chapter Four: The Search for a Vessel

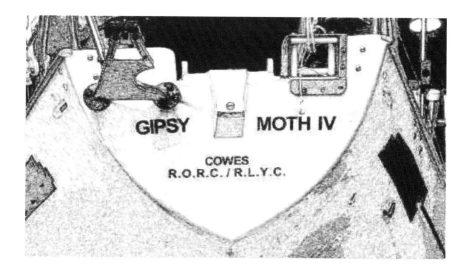

During the International Boat Show held at Earls Court, London, in January of 1968, *Gipsy Moth IV* co-designer Angus Primrose found himself buttonholed by a man he did not know – Donald Crowhurst, who was on-site selling Navicators. Although no-one had as yet heard of the *Sunday Times* race, which would not be announced till March, Crowhurst had already decided he wanted to join the number of contenders who'd previously announced plans to improve upon Chichester's accomplishment. In this connection, he petitioned Primrose – the wrong man, in fact, with no ownership interest or control over the vessel – for the use of Chichester's boat in his own attempt. (Ironically, Primrose's *Galway Blazer II* – which, as previously mentioned, he'd specially designed on commission from Bill King, and on which King would wind up competing with Crowhurst and others in the solo round-the-world race – was on display at the show.)

In return for having a somewhat capable vessel available for inexpensive loan rather than expensive purchase, Crowhurst seems to have been willing to ignore Chichester's own robust and loudly publicized criticisms of *Gipsy Moth IV*.

Primrose later said he'd been impressed by Crowhurst's self-confidence and what seemed, at least, to be his extensive yachting knowledge. (Crowhurst, all would agree, always talked a good game – not only to others, but to himself. As Stanley Best would recall: "[Crowhurst] seemed to have this capacity to convince himself that everything was going to be wonderful, and hopeless situations were only temporary setbacks. This enthusiasm, I admit, was infectious. But, as I now realise, it was the product of that kind of over-imaginative mind that was always dreaming reality into the state it wanted it to be.")

With regard to *Gipsy Moth IV*, other plans (and fundraising) were already well along to enshrine the vessel in permanent drydock at Greenwich, close by the *Cutty Sark*. Both Chichester and Lord Dulverton stood in favor of the project. But these facts did not deter Crowhurst. Once again addressing his plea to the wrong person, he wrote an expansive missive to the Town Clerk of Greenwich, in which the weekend sailor declared: " … I know myself to be competent to undertake this voyage in a seamanlike manner. I believe there is not a single hazard attendant upon my proposal that I have not considered, whether it may lie with the yacht, in the elements and sea, or in myself. There are risks in such a project, but I ask you to share them with me not only because they are acceptable but also because our tradition as a seafaring nation demands that we accept them." (In this one gets a good taste of the great rhetorical flare with which Crowhurst could often carry others, as well as himself, along.)

Not long after, when the Town Clerk told Crowhurst he had no power to say either yes or no, Crowhurst approached the *Cutty Sark* Society directly with the same argument, boosting this with an offer of a £5000 donation plus £10,000 in insurance. Given Crowhurst's strained financial situation, it is highly unlikely he had £5000 on hand, although he may have been able to scrape together the premium for the insurance. The Society, however, was not impressed. £17,000 had already been spent on the project, and the value of the boat alone far exceeded the numbers Crowhurst had mentioned. Unknown to Crowhurst, Chichester himself had voiced opposition after looking into Crowhurst's credentials as a sailor and finding them lacking.

After receiving several stern refusals, he sent one last letter to Frank Carr, chairman of the *Cutty Sark* Society's Ship Management Committee.

> *That you should have serious reservations about my ability to carry my plan through is understandable and indeed sound. A method by which the point may be proved would appear to be a short passage of a few hundred miles simulating single-handed conditions under observation. It would seem fair that two observers should be selected, one each. Obviously they must be men whose integrity and knowledge of the sea we can both accept, and I would readily*

agree to yourself as one should you wish it. If it seemed that I was endangering the yacht due to lack of skill, the observer could of course act as crew. The issue could be settled by the appropriate committee if a difference of opinion remained, though I would hope this was unnecessary.

Carr – most certainly under instructions from Chichester and Lord Dulverton – did not take up the offer.

Time marched on after the 17th March announcement of the race. Up until the second week of May, Crowhurst continued to argue that no other boat than *Gipsy Moth IV* would do – that he simply *must* have the vessel. But when he finally gave up on acquiring the use of Chichester's boat, he nearly immediately set his sights on an entirely different type of vessel – in fact one that could not have been more unlike what Chichester had taken round the world.

It is likely that both time and budget constraints impacted greatly on Crowhurst's decision when he suddenly became a devotee of trimarans. He'd never sailed one. But he knew two key things about the vessels: their per-bunk construction cost was approximately one-third of that for equivalent monohulls, and they could be built not only cheaply, but quickly. This latter attribute was perhaps the most major component of the equation, as by this time Crowhurst had only five months before the 31st October deadline for departure.

As with any vessel design, trimarans offer both advantages and risks. Comprised of a main hull and two outrigger hulls (or *floats*) to port and starboard, trimarans have no weighted keel, boast a great amount of sail-space relative to vessel size, and maintain stability in strong winds better than do monohulls. Also – given their advantageous sail to length-overall [LOA] ratio, their general lightness, and their shallow draft – they are capable of most excellent speeds, especially in straight-line performance. But the absence of a keel makes these vessels perform less than optimally to windward, not allowing sailors to come anywhere near as close-to-the-wind as is possible with monohulls.

Something else to be considered: A trimaran is far less likely than a monohull to capsize. On the other hand, on the rare occasion when a trimaran *does* turtle in a capsize, it usually stays turtled. Add to this the fact that the potential high speed of a trimaran can cause it to plow into the back of a wave and pitch-pole (flip over end to end).

Were a seaman to have adequate experience and training in a trimaran on the types of treacherous seas such as are found in the Southern Ocean, all of the risks associated with single-handing a trimaran through such waters would be acceptable, given the relative advantages of the craft. But Donald Crowhurst was not such a seaman – no matter what level his self-confidence. At the time Crowhurst converted to the church of trimarans, American Arthur Piver – an eminently experienced yachtsman and innovator of the "Victress" class of trimarans upon which Crowhurst's vessel would be based – had only recently been lost at sea while single-handing a Victress in the 1968 OSTAR (*Observer* Single-Handed Trans-Atlantic Race).

Chapter Five: The Caravan of the Sea

With magical thinking comes great audacity.

Crowhurst had been at odds with Stanley Best for several months. Best, having been patient with Crowhurst regarding repeated nonpayment of interest and principal on his loan, was now insisting upon the full return of his money, even if this meant liquidation of Electron Utilisation. Crowhurst, in turn, argued the prospects for a business turnaround, citing grand new innovations supposedly well-along in development and insisting all would be more than well in days ahead. Then, on 20th May, Crowhurst mustered the boldness, pluck, and (some might say) impudence to petition Best for even more money, this to be expended on Crowhurst's now fully-evolved scheme of circumnavigation aboard a trimaran.

The crux of Crowhurst's argument to caravan-dealer Best was the value his adventure would have in not only garnering prize-money, but also as a platform for showcasing electronics which could subsequently be marketed quite profitably on an exclusive basis by Electron Utilisation.

> *... The really exciting prospect is the possibility of a trimaran equipped with various safety mechanisms that I have designed for use in trimarans [which are] a highly suitable platform for ... electronic process control equipment.*
>
> *The trimaran is a light displacement craft built of marine ply and/or glass fibre. ... Interiors are spacious and well lit in comparison [to traditional yachts] and the continuation of the boating boom will ensure that the trimaran will become the caravan of the sea, once doubts about safety are removed. Apart from the fact that (to date) they stay capsized, they offer many other advantages over the keel boat, notably that they can be sailed about three times as fast, and that unlike a keel boat they are virtually unsinkable. If the practical utility of the equipment I propose can be demonstrated in such a spectacular way as in winning the* Sunday Times *Golden Globe and/or the £5000 prize and it is properly protected by patents, the rapid and profitable development of the company cannot be in any doubt. Let me say at this point that having been to sea in small boats over a period spanning almost thirty years you can rest assured that commercial considerations alone would not induce me to make this attempt. I have gone into the*

*problems and risks in detail, and am able to say that I am
confident of success ...*

*On the basis of the declared entrants I could win both
trophies, as I have already secured the approval of two
boatyards to a plan enabling work to begin at short notice on
a trimaran of well proven basic design with the necessary
self-righting features built in. My estimates indicate that the
boat would only cost about £6000 so that with yacht
mortgage facilities the outlay is very modest in comparison
with the returns, which do not merely accrue to this
company but include film rights, communications and story
rights and advertising revenue. The details I have given here
are known to very few people and are sought after by the
yachting press with some avidity, so I would ask for your co-
operation in treating them as confidential.*

Of course, Crowhurst's nautical experience was not thirty
years but in fact less than ten. And the closest he'd ever come
to "ocean" sailing was cruising on the Bristol Channel and
Celtic Sea on carefully selected Sunday afternoons, under
ideal weather conditions, usually with a crew of one or two
friends, on a monohull. What is more, the amazing electronic
devices to which Crowhurst alluded existed only in his head.
These included a "computer" which would avoid capsizes by
constantly monitoring unusual stresses in the rigging, rapid
changes in the wind-speed indicator, and other such warning
signs. At appropriate moments, the computer would automatically slacken sail to accommodate changing conditions. In
the event of a capsize somehow defeating this early warning
system, the same computer would activate and inflate a
buoyancy bag at the top of the mast. This in turn would stop

the boat from turning over completely, leaving it at an angle where it could be righted by the next favorable wave. A great idea. A great drawing on the back of a napkin.

Regardless of Crowhurst's theatrical admonition that Stanley Best keep details confidential, Donald himself issued a press release in which he described his equipment as already "operating successfully" in tests: the result of extensive longterm development efforts at Electron Utilisation. It all sounded very fool-proof – this despite the fact that on the day of Crowhurst's departure his "computer" would still be nothing more than a large pile of unassembled relays, transistors, and switches.

Best found himself left with the choice of either entirely abandoning his investment in Crowhurst's firm, writing this off as a total loss, or succumbing to Crowhurst's enthusiasm, investing more, and hoping against hope that this time Crowhurst's optimism might come to something. He chose the latter option. Per what Crowhurst promised, Best expected to lay out approximately £6000. But this amount was to double by the time of departure.

Best took two precautions. First, he insisted that Crowhurst also seek out other sponsors who might lessen the demand on Best's bank account. Secondly, he insisted that should Crowhurst not finish – should he retire for any reason mid-race – Electron Utilisation would be obligated to purchase the boat from Best. As both Best and Crowhurst understood, the effect of such a transaction would be the final and total bankrupting of Electron Utilisation.

Once financing had been arranged, time demanded that Crowhurst act quickly to complete construction and make his vessel sea-worthy. He would accomplish the first task, but not the latter. The crunch of time would prove disastrous to the sturdiness and safety of the trimaran. But at the end of May, the task still seemed manageable to the starry-eyed Crowhurst and those whom he carried along with him via his expansive rhetorical talent. The emperor wore no clothes, though no-one – not the least Crowhurst – could afford to notice.

At the time Crowhurst first seriously began planning his trimaran, both John Ridgway and Chay Blyth were all but ready to set off, with Knox-Johnston poised to depart not long after. Others were also well along in their preparations. By Crowhurst's math, given the speeds he'd be capable of in his trimaran, he'd still be able to beat every one of them in both the Golden Globe and the lapsed-time race even given a relatively late departure on the first day of October, thirty days before the 31st October deadline. The real race, to Crowhurst's mind, was the one of getting his vessel built and prepared in time. In the end she'd be built, but not well. And she'd in no way be ready for the voyage, even when he departed thirty days later than originally planned, on 31st October itself.

Chapter Six: Icarus With An Overdraft

There is a certain breed of people in this world whose bombastic, larger-than-life personalities, combined with their great confidence and eloquence, make them ideal carnival barkers, publicists, and entrepreneurs marketing the unusual and fantastic. Theirs is the art of exaggeration. Perhaps the best example of this select breed is P.T. Barnum, who masterfully orchestrated and promoted spectacles of all kinds, very few of them based in reality. These professional enthusiasts exude great energy and excitement when commissioned to do so, whether their focus be the marketing of a fantasy, the molding of a famous hero from mere mortal clay, or the romanticizing of a great but utterly impossible quest.

In Rodney Hallworth – known to friends as *Rodders* – Donald Crowhurst found a man talented in all three matters.

39 years of age when he met Crowhurst that June, Hallworth had "made his bones" – as the saying goes – as a journalist with the *Daily Mail,* where he focused on crime reporting. In that capacity he was perhaps best-known as the man who covered the 1956 case of suspected serial killer Dr. John Bodkin Adams. (He would later, in 1983, co-write a book on the topic.) He also, during her incarceration, developed a friendship with Ruth Ellis – the last woman to be hung for murder in Britain – and in fact accompanied her on her final walk to the gallows. After the *Daily Mail*, Hallworth served briefly as junior crime reporter for the *Daily Express* before leaving to start his own small publicity agency and news bureau in the quiet seaside environs of Teignmouth, Devon. In the midst of all this, he also wrote a rather well-done book entitled *The Last Flowers On Earth* (Angley Books, 1966) – this documenting the ill-fated 1966 Royal Navy East Greenland mountaineering expedition to Schweizerland.

A young protégé of the 1980s recalls Hallworth as "an irascible old bastard … with thick-rimmed glasses and an even thicker Stockport accent. … It was Rodney who taught me, time and time again, to write as if 'for the bloke in the pub'. To write news stories as if they were for my mates to hear. Or, even better, for some dumb drunk asshole who needs every stupid detail to be laid out in simple language."

A large man in both girth and personality, Hallworth was sometimes compared to Charles Laughton in the actor's role as Henry VIII – burly, loud, disheveled, garrulous, dogmatic, and constantly famished. His capacity for bitter was near legendary. Hallworth always resided at the center of the party – never showing a sign of drunkenness, never missing a thing, never losing control, never losing his uncanny knack for overstatement, and always on the alert for opportunity. But in years to come *Guardian* journalist Robert McCrumb would describe Hallworth, not inappropriately, as "a provincial hack ... who fed Crowhurst's fantasy life and persuaded him to headquarter his race campaign in Teignmouth. ... [Crowhurst] was Icarus, with an overdraft."

As its name implies, Teignmouth lies at the mouth of the River Teign. A fishing village in the 17th century, in Georgian times the village became a popular summer resort destination, which – along with its sister village of Shaldon to the south across the river estuary – it remains to this day. Teignmouth offers a pier full of amusements, moorings for pleasure craft, numerous hotels, and both river and sea beaches, the former giving bathers a splendid view of distant Dartmoor. The village is also an active port for tankers and freighters from around the globe, and hosts a small ship-building industry. A large red sandstone promontory on the Shaldon side of the estuary – called *The Ness* – forms the most definitive landmark for mariners approaching the port.

The noted 19th century seascape painter Thomas Luny (1759-1837) made his home at Teignmouth for some thirty years. Other notable residents have included the mathematician and originator of the first computer, Charles Babbage (1791-1871) – coincidentally a great hero of Crowhurst's.

In addition to being Hallworth's home, Teignmouth also served as one of his most important clients for whom he constantly worked every angle to get mentions in the national press, especially in the vital months of spring, just before the summer tourist season. (It was for this purpose that he once, when the town hall was under remodeling, arranged a meeting of the town council on the beach – the councillors fully decked out with wigs and other formal attire – creating a human interest story which travelled the length and breadth of Britain. Thus the promoter worked his magic, weaving something out of little more than nothing. This skill would come in handy *vis-a-vis* Hallworth's dealings with Crowhurst.)

Hallworth first learned of Crowhurst in late June when the *Sunday Times* commissioned his firm – the Devon News Agency – to get a photograph of the mystery man preparing a trimaran for the race. Upon returning, Hallworth's photographer mentioned that Crowhurst was apparently without a publicist. Hallworth and Crowhurst subsequently met at a hotel restaurant in Taunton. At first quite formal and gruff, Crowhurst quickly warmed to the gregarious, enthusiastic Hallworth. By the time the meal ended Hallworth had won appointment as press officer for Crowhurst's enterprise.

In place of an upfront fee, Hallworth would share in a percentage of any prize money or other remuneration arising from the voyage. Thus the price was more than right for Crowhurst.

Crowhurst showed Hallworth a chart he'd worked out which, in an ingenious combination of mathematical precision and magical thinking, "proved" that Crowhurst – given the enhanced performance capabilities of his customized trimaran – would inevitably win both the first-around and lapsed-time races, this despite leaving significantly later than other contenders. (Ridgway and Blyth had each already departed on 1st June, and Knox-Johnston on 14th June. Moitessier and Fougeron were projected to depart in mid-to-late July, and King at the start of August. For his part, Carozzo had barely begun work on his boat at Cowes. Crowhurst, meanwhile, at this point was still expecting a 1st October departure. Not a seaman himself, Hallworth was in no position to recognize Crowhurst's mathematics and assumptions as yet another exercise in self deception.)

In addition to publicity, Hallworth was to take on the task of finding commercial sponsors to help underwrite the venture. Up to this point, Crowhurst had been endeavoring to do this himself, with not much success. His results thus far: ten cases of Heinz tinned foods and a few bottles of Whitbread Barley Wine. (Ironically, Whitbread's tepid endorsement of Crowhurst would prove a forerunner to far more energetic yachting sponsorship by the brewery, this in the form of the Whitbread Round-The-World-Race – which many considered to be the "Grand Prix" of yachting events – held every four years through the 1970s, 80s, and early 90s, and featuring fully-crewed maxi-yachts.) Crowhurst's various other overtures to foil and container manufacturers, as well as battery makers, were to no avail.

For a start in gaining sponsors, Hallworth (exercising his role as publicist for the city of Teignmouth) offered to launch a fundraising drive there if Crowhurst would agree to start his voyage from the port, include Teignmouth in the name of the vessel, and in interviews before and after the voyage emphasize his exploit's relation to the seaside resort. Crowhurst had planned to name his boat *Electron*, after his firm. Now it became *Teignmouth Electron*.

Chapter Seven: The Dull Edge of Brilliance

Today the Brundall Marina is a quiet place of some 50 pleasure-boat berths located in Norwich on the River Yare, not far from the Norfolk Broads. But at the time with which we are concerned this was the location of the boatbuilding firm L.J. Eastwood, Ltd. The owners of the firm were the quiet, intense John Eastwood (in charge of boat design and construction) and the more outgoing John Elliot (in charge of publicity, sales, and ledger-sheets). Both men were in their thirties. While Elliot came from a business background, Eastwood came to the firm with extensive experience as a boatbuilder and designer for larger shops. Bearded, pipe-smoking, and contemplative, he boasted a reputation for quality work and rigorous, painstaking attention to detail. The quintessential perfectionist, he was not one to be rushed, nor to settle for the second-rate – not unless under great duress, and never willingly. But there was to be plenty of rush, duress, and unwilling compromise in the building of Crowhurst's vessel, nearly all of it the fault of Donald himself.

Eastwood's firm had in fact been Crowhurst's second-choice for the construction of the trimaran. He'd at first sought out the larger and better-established Cox Marine, Ltd. of Brightlingsea, Essex, to take on the job. Cox had already built a number of trimarans of the Victress class, and had the most experience with these vessels of any firm in Britain. Most importantly, their production line was already tooled to produce trimarans on quick schedules. However, Cox rebuffed Crowhurst, saying their current and back-ordered projects would prohibit them from even beginning his vessel before the end of October, let alone finishing it before a 1ˢᵗ October departure. What they could do, however, was construct the three trimaran hulls in short order on their existing production line, and deliver these to Eastwood's for final assembly. Thus the job was split between the two firms, with Eastwood's taking on what would prove to be the weightier part of the assignment. By all accounts, Eastwood's took on the job because they found themselves unhappily idle at the time, and also because the entrepreneurial Elliot thought publicity associated with building one of the boats for the round-the-world race would be well worth having.

Per Eastwood: Crowhurst's boat "was based on standard Piver-designed 'Victress' class hulls and crossarms, which provided an overall length of 41 feet (12.29 m), a waterline length (centre hull) of 38 feet (11.58 m), and a beam of 22 feet (6.7 m). But the remainder of the boat was designed specifically for Crowhurst's requirements, and departed in many respects from the standard specification."

From mid-June onward, an excited, ebullient Crowhurst bubbled with ideas for refining, improving, and customizing the Victress design for the round-the-world voyage, especially with regard to handling the violently crashing seas of the Southern Ocean. It was with the Southern Ocean in mind that Crowhurst and Eastwood drew plans which traded the Victress's standard high enclosed wheelhouse for a low "dog house" nearly flush with the deck, thus to strengthen the deck overall. This in turn severely limited the space available in the cabin, but Crowhurst thought it a reasonable trade-off for safety. In this he was correct.

The vessels of some other entrants represented designs which gave knowledgeable observers pause. Knox-Johnston's *Suhaili* featured a high deck-house which some thought would be no match for the Southern Ocean. The same went for Bill Leslie King's and Chay Blyth's nearly-identical production line yachts. In late June, when Commander Nigel Tetley of the Royal Navy entered with his own Victress trimaran, named *Victress* – which he'd owned and sailed and lived aboard for several years – commentators spoke with the same caution. Tetley's vessel featured the same high wheel-house Crowhurst and Eastwood had thought dangerous. But then Tetley was an experienced sailor and, unlike Crowhurst, would – despite this design flaw – wind up very nearly completing the round-the-world race as a legitimate winner of the lapsed-time race after having traversed the Southern Ocean quite successfully.

Eastwood said much later that he'd at first been impressed by Crowhurst's ingenuity: the extraordinary and remarkable originality of his ideas. Crowhurst's friend Peter Beard would recall how at the time of the planning of the Victress's customization, Crowhurst seemed "euphoric" and full of inventive energy. But Crowhurst's undoubted brilliance, Eastwood commented, had a "dull edge" which often rendered it useless. The man rarely seemed able to slice his way from theory to reality, from drawing board to execution. Elegant visions and designs meant nothing in the absence of the time and money needed to accomplish them. Crowhurst had a penchant for focusing on immediately *impossible* (or, at best, *improbable*) ambitions as opposed to immediately *achievable* ambitions, nearly always at the expense of the latter. As Eastwood would remember: "He kept having new ideas which were impossible to carry out and test in time, but which were often brilliant." A number of his modifications made sense. But – as shall be shown – time and budget-constraints were to render most of these moot.

In addition to dispensing with the high wheelhouse, Crowhurst and Eastwood also doubled the standard two box-section cross-arms connecting the hulls, these installed approximately four feet forward of the standard beam positions. The additional beams required extra watertight bulkheads to provide attachments. Thus two watertight collision bulkheads were added to each hull. Per Eastwood: "This multiplicity of bulkheads gave great strength, but resulted in an unusually large number of hatches – four in each wing hull and three in the centre hull – because of the reduction of access to storage compartments. The attachments of the crossarms to the bulkheads was made far stronger than usual. The number of bolts was trebled and instead of using washers, the load was spread by passing the bolts through continuous strips of heavy gauge stainless steel glued to the timber."

To further add "lateral rigidity," Crowhurst's and Eastwood's plans called for an innovative solution. Stresses in the rigging of a trimaran can sometimes bend upwards the extremeties of the crossarms. In response, Crowhurst and Eastwood planned to double the thickness of the upper surface of the box-section crossarms. Numerous other enhancements were introduced related to fastening rigging shrouds to the hull, and the general strengthening of the vessel overall. There were additional innovations, many of them interesting. But elegant plans mean nothing if not followed through – if not brought to life through excellence in execution. And this was not to be.

Chapter Eight: The Ill Founded Boat

The hull and floats arrived at Eastwood's on schedule: 28th July. After this, the schedule became a mirage, and the vessel a shambles. As has been indicated, the problem lay in the rushed nature of the project, which did not combine well with the need for innovation and attention to detail necessitated by Crowhurst's many variations on the standard Victress class specifications.

"The great tragedy of the *Teignmouth Electron* project from a marine engineering point-of-view," John Eastwood would write, "was that there was insufficient time to develop and test many advanced features of Crowhurst's original conception. ... Difficulties Crowhurst encountered on the voyage mostly involved aspects of equipment and fitting-out of a superficial nature that would have been cured if there had been adequate trials." Here, it must be emphasized, Eastwood is talking about Crowhurst's fundamental innovations to the hulls and other physical aspects of the vessel, rather than Crowhurst's illusory electrical devices – with which Eastwood and his crew had no involvement, and for which Crowhurst himself in fact never did any development beyond drawings.

In addition to innovations already detailed in the previous chapter, Crowhurst instructed that the floats' keels, stems, transoms, chines, and deck-to-hull joints be strengthened by adding extra layers of fiberglass. There were also further novel approaches adopted for reinforcing the attachment of the shrouds to the deck, and all shrouds and stays were increased in size. As well, the standard Victress main mast height of 42 feet (12.80 m) was reduced to 38 (11.56 m), in order to accommodate the weight of Crowhurst's buoyancy bag, and the mizzen mast reduced proportionally. (This latter change may well have helped exacerbate a problem Crowhurst would encounter throughout his voyage: poor performance into the wind.)

Teignmouth Electron's wardrobe of sails numbered 15 items: one Ghoster Genoa, one Reaching Staysail, two Yankee Jibs, two Large Jibs, two Working Staysails, one Working Jib, one Storm Jib, one Trysail, one No. 1 Mainsail, one No. 2 Mainsail, one No. 1 Mizzen, and one No. 2 Mizzen. Eastwood designed the sail plan himself when Crowhurst, by the end of August, had failed to procure the services of a professional rig designer (which Eastwood was not). The late design of the sails meant late delivery of the sails: one more factor contributing to make the 1st October departure date an illusion.

The journey from Woodlands to the Eastwood Yard took ten hours each way. "We were forever tracking up there to check on the progress," Clare Crowhurst told a *Daily Mail* reporter many years later. "The kids slept on a mattress in the back of our old van. Donald would be furious if they weren't working on the boat when he got there." But on nearly every occasion when work had stalled, it had stalled because Crowhurst – involved with a publicity party set up by Hallworth, or brushing up on his skills at a radio-telegraph course, or trying to work out plans so Electron Utilisation might eek out some revenue during his time away – was not available for consultations when it came time for crucial decisions to be made. In tandem with this, whenever Eastwood and crew decided to go forth and make changes without such consultations, Crowhurst became equally perturbed. Adding to tension was the fact that Eastwood denied a request from Crowhurst to try a standard Victress just being finished in the yard – a voyage which would have been his very first on a trimaran. The boat had been sold, and Eastwood did not feel he had authority to give Crowhurst his wish.

Several compromises in construction would prove absolutely critical.

First off, as previously mentioned, the watertight bulkheads specified by Crowhurst necessitated the use of several extra deck hatches: one for each compartment. To answer this need, John Eastwood designed a simple hatch of round wood, this to be bolted down to a soft rubber seal. But when the required soft rubber proved unobtainable in time for the departure, Eastwood used harder texture rubber which ultimately could not bend and mold correctly to the uneven deck. In other words, it could not form the desired seal.

Secondly, the heavy Onan gas-powered generator Crowhurst needed for charging his batteries mid-voyage wound up being installed in the worst of all possible places. As a sensible general rule to help avoid capsize, Crowhurst wanted all weighty equipment placed as low in the boat as possible, thus providing extra ballast. For this reason, Crowhurst instructed that the generator be installed in a compartment under the open cockpit – this despite the fact that generators need to be kept as dry as possible and the open cockpit would be subjected to the pounding down of constant waves through much of the voyage. As for a sealed hatch above the generator, bear in mind the problem with rubber noted in the previous paragraph.

Thirdly, Crowhurst's plan called for the vessel's Henderson Pumps to be deployed to suck bilge water (the result of what were expected to be mere minor leaks) out of all ten individual watertight compartments. Rather than run custom piping into each compartment, the plan was for Crowhurst to use an extended-length Heliflex hose which he'd insert into to each compartment individually. To handle the strong suction of the Henderson Pumps, however, that hose had to be double or triple strength in order to not collapse. In the end, the reinforced hose would not be gettable in time. Crowhurst would depart with standard strength hosing, and problems would ensue.

Lastly, Crowhurst's failure to get professionals to design a rigging plan in time had caused great delay in the laying of the deck. In their rush to get the project completed as quickly as possible, Eastwood's sought to expedite things by simply painting the deck with polyurethane paint rather than adhering to the standard Victress specification which called for the decks – like the hulls – to be sheathed completely in fiberglass. (Eastwood believed this would do, since he had doubled up on the thickness of the plywood decking.) When Eastwood tried to phone Crowhurst for approval, he could not reach him at his home. When the two men finally made contact, prep for the polyurethane had already begun. Crowhurst loudly voiced his disapproval – and even considered refusing delivery of the boat at this point. But the rush was of his own making, as were the consequences.

Of all the many issues which were to arise on the vessel, these four key problems and shortfalls were to prove the most catastrophic.

Despite chronic and well-founded concerns about delay, Crowhurst throughout the process made more and more work for the yard – thus continually threatening the already-unlikely schedule for completion – by issuing a non-stop barrage of change orders: the ripping out of already-installed cupboards which he replaced with open shelves for Tupperware containers; a special oversized rudder for extra control in the Southern Ocean; and other swirling revisions. Eastwood's men worked on a 70-hour week. Additional labor poached from other yards comprised a previously unknown night-shift. Heated arguments between Crowhurst and Eastwood became *de rigueur*. Meanwhile, many of the experienced boatwrights who'd been charged with assembling the vessel in such haste became increasingly – and not very confidentially – critical of her strength and utility. Eastwood himself would later – some said too much later – confess he had doubts the boat would do well in rough seas. (One experienced hand summed her up as: "A right load of plywood.")

A projected 31st August launching date came and went, as did the rescheduled 12th September launch date. When Crowhurst stiffly demanded that the finally projected 23rd September hold whatever the cost, Eastwood reminded him that the only thing lagging even more behind schedule than completion of the vessel was payment of invoices. Crowhurst's changes alone had racked up no less than £900 in additional charges. Ultimately, before Eastwood and Elliot would allow Crowhurst to sail the boat away on 2nd October, they'd demand a £1000 releasing fee – this only a portion of the total outstanding invoice. (The remaining balance included the construction costs for a boatshed [still standing] purpose-built for the construction of the vessel.)

Clare christened the vessel immediately before her launch on 23rd September – a month and one week before the deadline for departure. The champagne bottle did not break on her first attempt. All commented on the uselessness of nautical superstition: especially the one which took this particular event and marked it an ill-omen for both boat and crew. Nevertheless, there was shared excitement and joy as the vessel – tended by Crowhurst and a dozen others easing her with lines – slid down the ramp into the River Yare. Clare and Donald smilingly toasted each other and the mission – this despite the fact that only a week before she (in tears) had begged him to refuse delivery of the obviously inadequate vessel and cancel the entire adventure. He told her she was probably right, but he felt he had to continue even if he had to build the boat himself on the way round. A great slogan full of *do-or-die* certainty but – of course – nothing more than a slogan. Clare never asked again.

Crowhurst clearly thought his project too big a hole to climb out of without incurring utter and very public embarrassment, along with financial ruin. There could be no stopping.

Chapter Nine: Tempest Tossed

Final fitting-out took one week. Workmen stepped the mast, installed the rigging, and put on other finishing touches. Crowhurst and John Elliot, together with Crowhurst's friend Peter Beard and two workmen from Eastwood's, set off from Brundall on 2nd October, heading down the River Yare, thence to the North Sea, the English Channel, and Teignmouth. The distance between Brundall and Teignmouth is 222 nautical miles. Crowhurst's dismal voyage to cover this short distance took no less than two weeks, and was afflicted with mishaps from nearly the beginning, the first of these occurring even before *Teignmouth Electron* got out of the river.

It is very hard to get into trouble on the wide, calm Norfolk Broads of the River Yare, but there nervertheless are a few hazards. Crowhurst managed to find one of them rather quickly. At Reedham, an auto chain-ferry crosses the Yare. It was Crowhurst's luck that as he rode a fast ebbing tide while also motoring, the chain ferry began its movement across – the chains thus tightening and rising near the surface. Given the shallow draft of the trimaran, some aboard thought it safe to proceed. Crowhurst did not agree and, as the nominal *skipper*, made the decision to drop the anchor, thus bringing the vessel to a fast stop. But then the tide, which has no brakes, carried the trimaran round from its anchor, violently banging her into several pilings. The starboard float wound up holed.

After this, the weather turned foul. At Yarmouth, in the rainy and chill darkness, they found the swing bridge closed until morning. Given the height of her main mast, *Teignmouth Electron* could not pass even with the tide at its lowest ebb. Eventually four (it would seem, rather generous and gracious) bridge personnel were found at their homes and convinced to come and open the bridge. While waiting, the two workmen from Eastwood's patched the damaged float, after which they departed the vessel to return to Brundall, leaving just Crowhurst, Elliot, and Beard as crew.

Let's call it a voyage of discovery – in this case the discovery of flaws. One after another.

The sails had been incorrectly cut. Whenever not close hauled, the mizzen and main chafed on the shrouds. As well, the sails did not balance well. *Teignmouth Electron* proved even more uncontrollable to windward than would be expected from a vessel with no keel. In fact she could get no closer to the wind than 60°. In an unfavorable wind near Dover, the vessel took five hours to sail a mere ten miles, only then to be swept back by the tide as far as the Goodwin Light. Then followed three days of tacking back and forth between France and Britain, making only slow progress along the British coast in the process. On the fourth day Crowhurst and company used the trimaran's outboard to motor into the Suffolk Coast. Beard and Elliot disembarked at Newhaven, and Crowhurst and a reserve crew of two sent from Eastwood's began a two day wait for a gale to pass before pushing on. Once the gale dropped, Crowhurst and his new crew continued on for two more frustrating and slow days, eventually making Wootton Creek on the Isle of Wight.

Crowhurst continued single-handed to nearby Cowes, where fellow-competitor Alex Carozzo of Italy was busy overseeing finishing touches to his newly constructed 66-foot (20.11 m) ketch, *Gancia Americano* – this having been con-structed by the Cowes-based Medina Yacht Company. Like Crowhurst, Carozzo was a late entrant. In fact, construction on his vessel had commenced even later than construction on Crowhurst's boat. Unlike Crowhurst, however, Carozzo was a seasoned sailor and racer with a distinguished reputation and indisputable skills. And his boat – which had taken only seven weeks to build – was custom-made for single-handing. Not a few pundits thought Carozzo the most formidable entrant in the race, with the possible exception of France's Moitessier. Crowhurst spent a full day chatting with Carozzo. One wonders whether the Italian informed Crowhurst of the dim view he took of multihulls, having recently had a bad experience with one in the OSTAR.

Crowhurst departed Cowes on 13th October with a crew of one – a Cowes local and experienced sailor: Lieutenant-Commander Peter Eden, whom he'd just met. Eden would later note *Teignmouth Electron's* splendid performance (with speeds up to 12 knots) before the wind, but also her hideously bad performance in most other situations, especially to windward. Even good perforance brought problems. The vibrations of the high speeds caused the screws holding down the Hasler self-steering gear to repeatedly come undone. For some thirty-six hours they struggled against westerlies, tacking twice across the channel. Finally, on the 15th, the wind cooperated and blew the trimaran quickly to the Teignmouth harbor bar. Crowhurst made dock in the mid-afternoon. He had much to do, and his final deadline for departure remained the 31st.

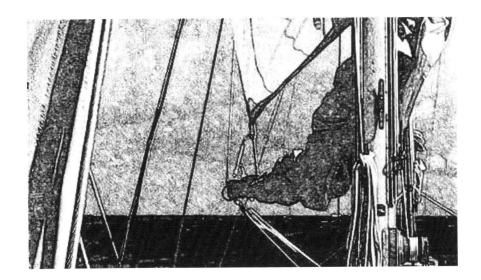

Chapter Ten: Teignmouth Underwhelmed

The echoes of Donald Crowhurst ring loud in Teignmouth to this very day. The 2010 obituary of longtime Teignmouth boatbuilder and harbor pilot Syd Hook made sure to mention that he "famously towed Donald Crowhurst's vessel the *Teignmouth Electron* out to begin its ill-fated round-the world adventure. Syd remarked at the time that Crowhurst was ill prepared for the [voyage]." Teignmouth's New Quay Inn, founded 1661, features a large mural portrait of Crowhurst on its exterior wall. It is said that Crowhurst's ghost wanders the waterfront on foggy nights.

One year before Crowhurst came to town , the Beatles – in the midst of filming their *Magical Mystery Tour* – had occupied the best suite at the Royal, this being Teignmouth's premier hotel. Now Crowhurst and his family moved in, courtesy of the Teignmouth Chamber of Commerce. *Teignmouth Electron*, meanwhile, got hauled-out at the prestigious Morgan Giles

Shipyard. There a crew dispatched from Eastwood's – aided by Morgan Giles staff – continued to do their best to make the trimaran ready.

Founded in 1921 by noted Naval architect and yacht designer Francis Charles Morgan Giles (OBE), the Morgan Giles Shipyard had a wide reputation in yachting circles for the creation of a range of superior vessels, many of them destined to become classic designs. Francis Charles Morgan Giles died in March of 1964, at the age of 81. The *Times* noted: "With the death of Morgan Giles, the world of yachting has lost one of its best known characters. He was perhaps the last survivor of the almost legendary band of great English yacht designers from the early years of this century – from the days of Fife, Nicholson and Mylne." At the time Crowhurst and *Teignmouth Electron* arrived there, the yard was near the end of its days but nevertheless still boasted many of the very finest shipwrights to be found in all of England.

"When Donald Crowhurst arrived in Teignmouth," remembers a local, "his boat was in a shocking state, and he, according to my father, didn't seem much better either. When a press event was called at the Royal Hotel, my father was invited (as was anyone else with a few quid) in the hope that money would be donated towards the great hope of Teignmouth. I remember asking him the next day whether he had parted company with any cash, and he said not on your life, and that in his opinion Crowhurst wouldn't get as far as Torquay. Many of the staff at Morgan Giles's spent much time and effort beyond the call fo duty trying to make [Crowhurst's boat] seaworthy, and received little thanks for their efforts. Many years later I asked one of them why, and he said they had felt sorry for Crowhurst, and simply wanted to help him out, although he also said that he now greatly regretted having done so, believing that if they hadn't made the boat reasonably fit to go, Donald Crowhurst would indeed not have made it to Torquay, which might well have saved his life."

The Morgan Giles shipwrights were somewhat out of their element in trying to improve *Teignmouth Electron*. They weren't experienced in bandaging poorly built vessels; they'd spent their entire lives building first-rate vessels from scratch. Remedial measures were not their forte. What is more, they – just like the men who had come from Eastwood's – had a hard time communicating with the distracted and aloof Crowhurst, who as the days wore on towards the deadline seemed to become increasingly numbed by the magnitude of tasks and worries with which he had to deal. He was a man on the brink of jumping from a very high cliff with a parachute stitched hastily from rags; and he seemed to know it.

Crowhurst had not even begun to work on the various electronic gizmos which he'd long claimed would make *Teignmouth Electron* a truly revolutionary boat. Even the standard-issue Marconi Kestrel radio had yet to be installed. Meanwhile, the so-called "watertight" hatch in the cockpit floor had proven itself to be *anything but* watertight during the maiden voyage. Now some low rubber-edged combing was added to the original combing on this and other hatches in the hope this would solve the problem. There was no time for a more extensive revamp. Numerous other wounds and infections – such as the screws holding down the Hasler gear – received band-aids, but little more. The entire two weeks prior to Crowhurst's departure was one long exercise in *making-do*.

Things were not much better on the ground. Hallworth had done a pathetic job of gathering patrons. The "Name it *Teignmouth*" fund he'd started, with a goal of raising £1,500, had garnered only £250. So far as supplies went, the publicist had gathered contributions in the way of stores of Exeter Cheese and sherry from a local maker – but that was about it.

There had, from the start, been a high level of skepticism in Teignmouth regarding Hallworth's enthusiasm for Crowhurst's project. This increased dramatically in the two weeks the townspeople had to study Rodney Hallworth's proffered stranger/hero. This was especially the case among watermen – Teignmouth's many shipwrights, sailors, dockworkers, and fishermen. These were men who knew the sea and respected it, men who recognized a carpetbagger and tourist when they saw one, men who respected thoroughness, rigor, and professionalism, and who understood the world's oceans as being serious places not hospitable to dilettantes. Their skepticism of Crowhurst was only matched by their skepticism regarding his boat.

John Norman and a camera-crew from the BBC interviewed locals, many of them scornful at the sight of Crowhurst's clearly disorganized – in fact *frantic* and disorganized – effort to make final preparations. Morgan Giles workers grumbled about the flood of contradictory instructions emanating from Eastwood, Elliot, and Crowhurst. Confusion increasingly replaced logic. The whole shipyard became a study in chaos. Looking back many years later, Crowhurst's son Simon recalled his own impressions at the time even as an eight year old: "The boat wasn't ready, and there was the tension and the sense of something approaching doom that was in the air."

The BBC filmed two fishermen in a conversation where they chuckled and made clear their opinion while gazing out at *Teignmouth Electron* from shore, shortly before her departure:

> *"My idea, in a gale of wind, you'd want something in which you could snuggle down and heave-to. But I don't see how you could heave-to in a thing like that."*
>
> *"There's nothing in the water to counteract the force of the wind. You'd just blow away before the wind, blow to leeward all the time."*
>
> *"He'll have to spend half his time broadside on."*
>
> *"Go round the world sideways!"*

In a lengthy interview with Donald Kerr and John Norman, Crowhurst startled his inquisitors by answering questions as though he had already completed the voyage, and had long experience with extended, single-handed sailing. "Talking to yourself is very important. When one has been awake for a couple days, soaking wet and perhaps hadn't had enough to eat ... you can restore a sense of urgency by telling yourself what the consequences of your lack of attention are." The most extended of voyages Crowhurst had ever made in his life was the one *with crew* from Brundall to Teignmouth, and there is no record of him even spending a single overnight "at sea" prior to this. Nevertheless, Crowhurst's confident tone mimicked the heroic bravado of a Shackleton or a Hillary. What Crowhurst lacked in expertise and experience, he certainly made up for in rhetoric.

On 26th October, Crowhurst took his boat out for final trials. John Elliot, the BBC's John Norman, and a BBC cameraman joined him. Once again, things did not go well. Crowhurst had hoped his vessel, now weighted down with supplies and thus digging slightly deeper into the sea, would perform better to windward. She didn't. She repeatedly refused to come about, causing Crowhurst and Elliot to have to back the jib on more than one occassion. It was a two man job. Crowhurst wouldn't be having any such help going forward. Also on this day, the attachments for the running foresail sheets began lifting from the deck as soon as those sails were raised – positing a very bad situation in the case of high winds. More good news: the reinforced rubber deck sealing on hatches proved useless. Water soaked through. And the rubber combing actually fell away when Crowhurst raised the key hatch in the cockpit floor. Countless other details threatened as well.

The BBC presence was part of a coverage arrangement Rodney Hallworth had cut with the broadcasting corporation. "We negotiated a contract with Rodney Hallworth," Donald Kerr would recall. "It was a very small contract. £250 and another £150 when the film was delivered at the end of the race. We didn't know how it was going to turn out: whether this was just going to be a few hundred feet of film from a man who got part way around the world, whether we were dealing with a potential winner, or whether it was just going to be a nice feature film showing life at sea. So, it was left open. If

Donald Crowhurst succeeded and the film was good, he would be paid considerably more." As part of the contract, Kerr and Norman supplied Crowhurst with an inexpensive 16 mm camera and appropriate sound recording equipment – both of which he quickly mastered, even though this was the least of his concerns.

On the eve of departure, the boat remained a shambles, and Crowhurst's buoyancy bag and computers nothing more than wishful fabrications: smoke, mirrors, and unassembled spare parts. The buoyancy bag sat atop the mast, but its wiring led down through the mast to nothing but open space, dangling from the roof of the small cabin. As we've seen, key fastenings were already coming away during relatively calm passages along the British coast. What is more, Crowhurst himself seemed as broken and confused as his vessel. His normal bravado had by now fallen away, and only reappeared during those moments when he spoke to a journalist or performed for a news camera. All his intimates – most especially Clare – noticed the change in his mood: the wistful fatalism which now seemed to cloak him. He felt he had no way out: especially after a conversation with Hallworth and Best during which both – with mere monetary skin in the game vs. Crowhurst's literal skin – insisted he absolutely had no option but to proceed. To cement things, Stanley Best – on this, Crowhurst's last full day on land – forced Crowhurst to sign papers giving Best a second-mortgage on the Crowhurst family home, Woodlands, in order to secure the money Best had so far expended. Thus, if Crowhurst retreated, he'd not only confront great national embarrassment and a bankrupt business, but also a homeless family.

John Elliot said later that in private conversation he warned Crowhurst not to go. But to this Crowhurt responded he was past that. It was too late. He could not turn back. Donald Kerr remembers Crowhurst "quivering from lack of sleep and food. … He knew [the voyage] would kill him, but he could never quite bring himself to say so." Kerr was so concerned that on the final day of preparations he told his crew to stop filming and instead do what they could to help with the last-minute loading and sorting of supplies. *Herald Express* reporter John Ware summed things up: "The trimaran was a bit of a leaky tub, and there was no hope of it being fitted out properly. … Many of us had strong doubts that it would stand up to a real pounding, and Crowhurst, deep down, knew he wasn't really ready. But he had little choice. Not sailing would have meant financial ruin and public humiliation … ."

"That last night together was frightful," Clare told *Daily Mail* reporter David Jones in 2006. "We were both in a terrible state. I had never seen Donald crying before, except when his friend was killed in an air crash, but he was really weeping. I held him in my arms and comforted him. Neither of us slept at all." She believes it was worry about finances which made him continue despite all evidence that this might well be suicide. "To Donald, taking care of the family meant everything, and he was desperately worried because that day Stanley Best had him sign a last-minute agreement stating that the house would be mortgaged if the boat was lost, or he gave up the race. … I still feel so incredibly guilty about it. I think if I had just said 'This is barmy! Stop it!' he would have listened. But I was scared that in five years' time, he'd have regretted not going, and I would have stopped him fulfilling his dream."

Chapter Eleven:
A Sort of Pinpoint on the Horizon

On the morning of departure day, Hallworth lured Crowhurst to a waterside chapel for the taking of publicity photos. The resulting images show our reluctant hero kneeling and meditating. An athiest, he refused to pray to a diety he did not believe existed. It is said there are no athiests in foxholes – but evidently the saying is wrong.

At 3 PM, fans waved from shore as harbor pilot Syd Hook towed *Teignmouth Electron* over the harbor bar. A cold, light rain fell, just as it had all the week before. Three boats accompanied the trimaran: friends (including Crowhurst's family), officials, the BBC. The first problem took only minutes to materialize. Men (Eastwood's men, rather than those from Morgan Giles) had attached the jib and staysail to the wrong stays. Additionally, in the midst of hurriedly affixing the moot buoyancy bag to the top of the mast the day before, workers had lashed the bag to two adjacent foresail halyards. Thus Crowhurst found himself ignominiously being towed back to dockside. Now a Morgan Giles workman climbed the mast and fixed the lashing, while Crowhurst himself tended to the other matter. Then another tow and, finally, at 4:52 pm (plus five seconds), Crowhurst raised his sails and officially crossed the start-line.

Boats followed for a mile or so before turning back. "About five o'clock at night it was," Hallworth recalled. "A gray sky started to die, and he just finished up a sort of pinpoint on the horizon. Then we all came back and we never saw him again." Simon Crowhurst comments: "I remember vividly the effort of trying to see the sail for as long as possible, of watching that sail getting smaller and smaller and waving, occasionally, just in case he could see us, and, finally, straining to see it even after it had completely disappeared."

Crowhurst, making his first recording for the BBC, would comment: "I have never put to sea in such a completely unprepared state in my life. Nevertheless, the stipulations were that competitors would leave by the 31st, and leave by the 31st I did." In fact, he'd never "put to sea" ever before in his life – *period*. Back at Cowes, the much better-organized, equipped, and knowledgeable Carozzo also felt not fully prepared as the deadline approached. His solution, however, was to simply cast off before midnight on the 31st, then anchor in the harbor for several days, getting his boat in order, under supervision to make sure no one boarded or rendered any form of assistance while he did so. But then, Carozzo's last minute details were, in fact, details – and no-where near as formidable as the myriad problems which confronted Crowhurst.

Where were the other competitors at the point when Crowhurst set out?

As previously noted, John Ridgway had departed Inishmore – one of the Aran Islands, 40 miles off the coast of Ireland – in his weekend cruiser *English Rose IV* on 1st June – the first allowable day of departure according to race rules. His boat promptly proved itself not up to the demands of the race. Ridgway and a battered vessel retired from the race on 21st July, pulling into the Brazilian port of Recife. Chay Blyth departed in his production-line yacht on 8th June. On 15th August he technically disqualified himself when he accepted an invitation at Tristan da Cunha to step aboard an anchored cargo ship. Nevertheless, he continued to sail for his own enjoyment, briefly. Soon his inadequate vessel began to fall apart beneath him, and he finally – after sailing the length of the Atlantic and around Cape Agulhas – retired at the port of New London on 13th September.

Also as previously stated, Robin Knox-Johnston had sailed from Falmouth in his *Suhaili* on 14th June. Moitessier and Fougeron departed on Thursday, 22nd August, and King two days later. Tetley, skippering the only other trimaran in the race, set off 16th September, a week before Crowhurst launched *Teignmouth Electron* in Norfolk. On 31st October, Fougeron – running a few hundred miles behind King – had just passed Tristan da Cunha. Both men found themselves in the midst of a severe storm on the 31st – one which damaged their boats to an extent that they both shortly had to retire. On the same date, Moitessier was already two days into the Southern Ocean. Meanwhile, Knox-Johnston had passed Cape Leeuwin and was well down Australia's southwestern coast. Tetley was approaching Trinidade.

To summarize, as Crowhurst set out, the race had already winnowed down to just five contenders: Knox-Johnston, Moitessier, Tetley, Crowhurst, and Carozzo.

Crowhurst – exhausted – took things easy for the first day or so, heading southeast out of Lyme Bay, then back in the direction of Torquay, and then southeast once more. Some 24 hours into his voyage he passed the Eddystone Light. Leaving much to the boat's self-steering, he slept and then spent many hours sorting through the chaos of gear and supplies strewn about the boat's compact cabin, putting things in order. Vast amounts of dried foods filled up scads of Tupperware containers, most of these tucked into various bulkheads – providing both storage and buoyancy.

He also dealt with the boat's first issues, which commenced promptly. The foresail halyards somehow became knotted. He was still in British waters, just off Falmouth, when his Hasler self-steering gear – designed for monohull top speeds rather than multihull top speeds – became problematical. As they had earlier, two key screws came loose due to vibrations. Crowhurst, incredibly, had not thought to pack replacement screws or bolts. Thus began his cannibalization of *Teignmouth Electron* – swiping screws from less crucial gear. This was a maddening process which would repeat itself time and time again. But it was Tuesday, 5th November, when even more serious trouble first showed its face.

Crowhurst's port bow float became completely flooded to deck level. He fought to bail the compartment over the course of three hours, while at the same time shipping water amid waves 15 feet high and a wind blowing Force 7. A grueling task. Once this was done he screwed the hatch down with a Syglass fiberglass casket, in hopes this would solve the problem. It didn't. (It is worth noting that Clare had spotted signs of this impending problem some two weeks before and told Donald who, besieged by other issues, shook it off as irrelevant. He could only absorb so much bad news, and confront so many obstacles, at one time. But denial could prove deadly at sea.)

On the 7th, he took stock of his progress over the previous four days. His logline showed great speeds, approx. 134.5 miles a day for a total of 538. However, his actual progress was a mere 290 miles (72.5 miles per day), as he – with his limitations to windward – had burned much time tacking into a wind blowing hard from the south. This was not the impressive rate of advance Crowhurst had been counting upon.

While confronting his mounting issues, he at the same time put on a brave face in sections of his logbooks where he adopted a properly strenuous, cheerful, and optimistic voice. In passage after passage he mimicked the strident, heroic, cheery tones he'd encountered in reading the logs and memoirs of other properly British heroes. Here were all the expected themes and tropes: the value of discipline, the company of dolphins and other sea creatures, the beauty of solitude, the kinship and communion with long-gone navigators of yore, the art of cooking tasty dishes and accomplishing other domestic tasks under less than optimal conditions, and so forth. All of it rehearsed, stilted, trite. All of it great showmanship. All of it probably meant for publication. Only occassionally was he blunt about his problems, and appropriately enraged and pessimistic. Only in these few dark passages did he – according to friends who read the logs once all was done – sound like his true self rather than an actor playing a role.

True disaster struck on the 13th. On a heading to westward in a southern gale, the still-faulty cockpit hatch demonstrated its uselessness in a grand way: the engine compartment below the cockpit flooded completely, putting the Onan electric generator underwater. So where was Crowhurst now? His overall buoyancy was threatened by leaks in the outrigger hulls. And now this. Should he have been surprised? No. The cockpit hatch had proved worthless on his first voyage from Brundall to Teignmouth, and then the "solution" applied had been plainly inadequate on his last trial before departure. Much earlier, Eastwood had warned him that the hatch, due to its positioning, would be vulnerable. So Crowhurst now suffered the double indignity of facing a serious problem *and being proved incompetent*. Perhaps, after all, he should have trusted a professional boatbuilder to know something about building boats.

With these mounting problems, just two weeks into his journey, Crowhurst for the first time (according to his log) contemplated the prospect of having to abandon his voyage. He summarized the state affairs in an extended and eminently honest logbook entry on the 15th. After two weeks at sea, he'd logged some 1,300 miles but had in fact advanced only 800 miles over a course of some 30,000 miles. Miserable progress overall.

There were many matters to consider.

The loss of the Onan meant he'd likely not be able to transmit, thus creating a situation where he would not be able to get in touch with others (most importantly Clare, who would be terrified by the silence) were he unable to rectify the problem. The loss of electric also meant no hope of making the masthead buoyancy bag functional, no time signals, no light. What's more, the leaking of the cockpit hatch seemed incurable. 75 gallons accumulated overnight. He thought one approach at a remedy might be to screw and seal the hatch down permanently, but he vetoed this because it would deny him vital access to the electrics. Plus he would not have the option of pumping out any accumulated water.

And yet there was more.

His Hasler self-steering gear – not really devised with vessels such as the multihull *Teignmouth Electron* in mind – underperformed, succumbing to wild breaches which would likely mean inevitable death in the big seas of the Southern Ocean. Given his late start and his slow progress, he'd likely arrive at the Horn at a particularly dangerous time: April/May. To do so without adequate self-steering, let alone a functional buoyancy bag, was unthinkable. He also lacked the capacity of pumping water from the leaky bilges – for he'd in the past few days realized the hoses stowed were inadequate to handle the suction of the Henderson Pumps. Thus a great deal of strenuous manual bailing would be required, especially in high seas when the tiller simply could not go unmanned. An unsolveable issue. Smaller problems also loomed – none of them fatal, but completely disasterous when taken in their totality.

With these issues summarized, Crowhurst went on to ponder his alternatives: both realistic and not. He contemplated Stanley Best – the only man he'd have to convince of anything – perhaps being open to abandonment of the current voyage and deferral until August, at which time Crowhurst would set off again, properly prepared, with a view toward beating any record for fastest solo circumnavigation that might be set by any of the current contenders. He also considered the option of proceeding as far as Australia (or perhaps less ambitiously, Cape Town) and in one of those places retiring with honor – hoping all along that this demonstrated effort would assuage Best and put his benefactor off invoking those clauses of their agreement which would effectively bankrupt both Electron Utilisation and Crowhurst.

Given the abdications of Ridgway, King, and Blyth, Crowhurst calculated that retirement to anywhere from Cape Town or beyond would at least not involve abject humiliation. Ultimately he decided to push south while continuing to consider his options: none of them appealing. At the same time he intended to try to repair the generator and then talk to Best and assess his views so far as retiring was concerned.

But he continued to be a magical thinker, fully believing he could beat any record with another attempt one year later. And he congratulated himself on having launched off on his journey just four and a half months after the start of construction – seemingly ignoring the fact that he'd set sail in something suited more to a fools' rules regatta than a strenuous round-the-world race. He wrote further that he refused to accept "superficial" assessments of failure and, remarkably, compared his situation to that of Christ, who emerged ultimately victorious after dying on a cross between two thieves. But for Crowhurst there was to be no Ressurection.

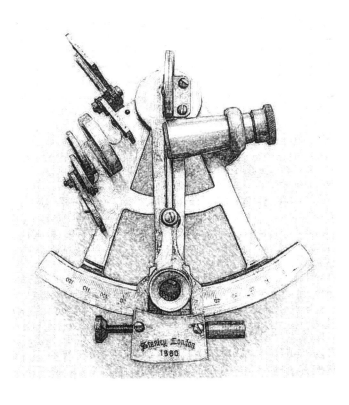

Chapter Twelve: Deceit

Crowhurst grew a closely-cropped goatee, along with a moustache. His face hardened and thinned. He used the BBC camera to record himself performing random tasks: setting the jib, steering, and holding a halyard while giving viewers a jaunty thumbs-up. The clips show us someone who seems a completely confident man: a man in-charge, a master of his vessel and a natural conqueror of the elements going busily about the work of great achievement – achievement such as most mere mortals would never know. Here was the romantic lone hero. Here was the cheerful adventurer, afraid of nothing. But in fact he was the most desperate of men – a man daunted by his broken vessel, by fate, by shoreside economics, and by the vast, forbidding oceans with which he found himself confronted.

He managed to get his generator working on the 16th, even though the fundamental problem of water leaking in from the cockpit hatch, and salt impacting the battery performance, remained unsolved, thus making the fix fragile and quite temporary. With power restored, Crowhurst cabled Hallworth with an implied lie about his location. He was, he telegraphed vaguely, "going towards" Madeira.

Technically true, in the same way that a hiker who sets out westward from Manhattan is "going towards" Ohio. In this, as in subsequent cables, Crowhurst pointedly gave no precise information about his location, but instead simply named a destination. The subtext seemed to be that he was past the Azores and nearing Madeira, when in fact even the Azores were several hundred miles beyond where he found himself. Hallworth made the assumption Crowhurst must have expected, and told the press his client was "near Madeira." Ironically, even Crowhurst's falsely implied progress reflected a fairly lousy rate of speed for a trimaran: fewer than 100 miles per day. But still, this pathetic report played better than reality, which was roughly half that.

Making his chart many months before, comparing vessels and calculating probabilities, he'd estimated his average daily rate of progress at 220 miles. Now, using an equally unreal estimate of between 60 and 90 miles per day, he devised a very different chart designed to help him see if he could possibly make it to Australia, or even just past the Cape of

Good Hope, before April or May, when the southern winter would make either passage impossible for Crowhurst's increasingly fragile craft. The answer was *no*.

As he noted in a logbook meditation, his two best options were either to push down the African coast to Cape Town, probably arriving there by May, or to simply head west across the Atlantic through relatively safe waters near shipping lanes, and take *Teignmouth Electron* to the United States where he guessed he could sell her for a decent price. But he still had magical thoughts. In the same paragraph he considered that he might simply turn around and embark upon a "record breaking" return trip to England (somehow logging speeds he could never in reality hope for no matter the direction), and thereby achieve a conquest which would negate his failure to complete the round-the-world voyage.

Amid this sea of unfriendly and unsurmountable facts, unreality became more and more appealing by the moment. Interestingly, in a radio-telephone-call of the 17th during which he spoke to both his wife and Stanley Best, he did not mention any of his problems save for the pumping issue, and made no noises about either quitting or turning about. He also lied about his position, saying he was 100 miles off Madeira. It seems as if in the previous 24 hours or so he had moved into a new phase of his project. After many months of deceiving himself, he now moved on to Act Two: deceiving others.

For three days thereafter he did nothing. He apparently hovered north of Madeira, his boat swimming in slow circles which carried him only about 180 miles south overall.

What were the other contestants doing at about this time? Carozzo had been forced to retire at Lisbon due to a stomach ulcer. Knox-Johnston was just off New Zealand. His boat had been smashed and battered by the stormy seas of the Southern Ocean, but he'd bandaged his half-destroyed self-steering gear and rudder, and soldiered on, beating Chichester's claim to having accomplished the longest non-stop solo voyage. Tetley was near the Cape of Good Hope, and had already broken the record for the longest solo voyage in a multihull. Moitessier was not far behind Knox-Johnston. And Fougeron, his boat badly damaged in a capsize, had decided to call it quits.

Annotations in Crowhurst's *Pilot* books suggest he strongly considered putting in at Madeira's capital, Funchal. But he did not mention this possibility, nor the long list of problems he'd noted down in a script for a second phone call, when he spoke once again to Stanley Best. He had, it seems, come up with another solution. After discussing several inconsequential problems with Best, he closed off the call with a warning that due to the ongoing problem with the cockpit hatch and the continued flooding of the Onan generator there might well be extended radio-silence going forward. But a day or so later he sent a chipper telegram to Hallworth: "TUNING TRIALS OVER … RACE BEGINS."

During the last week of November or the first week of December he moved out of the prevailing westerlies and into the following winds of the North-East Trades. Given these favorable conditions, one is almost tempted to believe the startling, suddenly-magnificent mileages he reported to Hallworth in a cable of 10th December.

PRESSE – DEVONNEWS EXETER
HURTLED SOUTH   FRIDAY 172   BROKE JIB POLE
SATURDAY 109   SUNDAY 243   NEW RECORD
SINGLE HANDER   MONDAY 174   TUESDAY 145
NORTH EAST TRADE FINISHED

The horse with the broken leg was suddenly, miraculously, a contender. Crowhurst confirmed the distances in a radio-telephone-call with Hallworth on the 11th, and provided details. In a quote given by Hallworth to the *Sunday Times*, Crowhurst said of his record-setting day: "It took pretty strong nerve. I have never sailed so fast in my life and I could only manage speeds of up to 15 knots because the sea was never higher than 10 feet. If I get the chance again and the seas run any higher I doubt if I will take it because it might prove too dangerous." The *Times* article – quizzically headlined *Crowhurst Speed World Record?* – noted: "The achievement is even more remarkable in the light of the very poor speeds in the first three weeks of his voyage; he took longer to reach the Cape Verdes than any other competitor."

Not everyone believed in miracles. Francis Chichester said privately that Crowhurst's recovery seemed suspect, and that a close examination of his navigational record would be in order upon his return. *Sunday Times* navigational advisor Captain Craig Rich, of London's School of Navigation, expressed similar concerns.

On 17th December Crowhurst cabled Hallworth that he was over the Equator. He wasn't. He was 190 miles north of there. Three days later, he announced that he was averaging a daily speed of 170 miles. All fine, heroic stuff. But in fact, on that particular day, Crowhurst's mileage was 13 – which makes sense, considering he was in the infamous Doldrums. Roughly 700 miles wide, the Doldrums lie along the Equator smack in between the trade-wind corridors of the Northern and Southern Hemispheres, and are known for their eerie calms and erratic winds. Knowledgeable sailors – Chichester and Rich among them – thought Crowhurst's high speeds here to be especially remarkable, and especially suspect.

Long after the race had ended and Crowhurst was dead, John Ridgway would confess to having contemplated fraud in lieu of retirement. He said he'd "considered the idea of simply resting in the sun for a year and then returning home to say that I had been all the way round the world." This, on the face of it, would seem preferable to the humiliation of defeat and the disappointment of friends and supporters who had worked so hard to help him get underway. But Ridgway quickly discounted the idea. "First, I doubted if it could be carried off, too many people would see through the story. Second, and more important, it would not be possible for me to live with such a fabrication."

Ridgway was right. It could not, in the end, be successfully carried off. But in the throes of his latest mania, and the exuberance of a freshly-sparked round of magical thinking, Crowhurst would not have considered this. Or if he did consider it, he presumed he had the skills to build a believable narrative not just of words, but of numbers: a watertight navigational record with accurate calculations, sun sights, and weather conditions in all the right imagined positions on all the right days, these nesting nicely beside any location details he might transmit on an given date: complete synchronization of navigational and radio logs. Fabricated spherical geometry at its utmost complexity. This would have been no mean feat, but Crowhurst evidently believed himself up to the task.

Chapter Thirteen: Alone

Crowhurst was now not only isolated physically, but emotionally. Just him alone with his secret. His lie. His deceit. And utterly so. With nothing and no-one to rely on other than his fabulations and his broken vessel. But he seemed not to care

On Christmas Eve he made a pre-arranged radio-telephone-call to Clare. At Hallworth's request, she pressed for a clear statement of Crowhurst's exact position: longitude and latitude. This he did not provide, explaining that he'd not as yet had a chance to take sun sights that day. What he did do, however, was tell the most fantastic of his lies thus far. He stated that he was somewhere off Cape Town. He was, in fact, *considerably* off Capetown: some 3,000 miles to the west. (A Christmas note he'd packed away from his friend Peter Beard read in part: "At a guess I would say you're off the Canary Islands. How far out am I?" If Beard only knew.)

That night, Crowhurst switched on his BBC tape recorder and struck a pose: easily slipping into his public personna of the stoic lone voyager bravely and selflessly confronting the great depths of the world's oceans in a quest to achieve something noble. He opened by playing "Silent Night" on his mouth-organ. Then …

> *Oh, it's a beautiful and melancholy carol, and although it's not terribly well played, there is something in that very amateurishness … evocative of the situation of loneliness and peril … . It's the sort of instrument that in the blitz somebody would play, or in a dugout during a bombardment … .*
>
> *Not that I'm under any great stress, but there is something rather melancholy and desolate about this part of the Atlantic Ocean, and it's fitting somehow that I should be playing a mouth-organ on Christmas Eve. … One thinks of one's friends and family, and one knows that they're thinking of one, and the sense of separation is somehow increased by the – by the loneliness of this spot and, well, the sound that I've just made is representative in many ways of the ethos of the occasion. Anyway, enough of it – let us have something merry.*

With that, Crowhurst returned to the mouth-organ and kicked out a fast, jolly version of "God Rest Ye Merry Gentlemen." But the only mention he made of God was in the unsung lyrics of the two carols. God was not to be found on

Teignmouth Electron. Nor was humility.

Abroad on his *Suhaili* about this same time, Robin Knox-Johnston pondered the "colossal natural forces" of wind and sea and, like generations of mariners before him, considered their genesis. "However practical you think you are," he would write, "the feeling comes that there is more to it all than natural laws, and if you have been brought up in a society that bases its philosophy upon the existence of a Superior Being, you come to consider that this Being is responsible, and to accept that He exists." One certainly had to do the work of one's own well-being and survival both at sea and on land, but: "When everything has been done that you know you can do, you put your trust in your Superior Being, and just hope that what you have done is right. … Because of this belief, throughout the voyage I never really felt I was completely alone, and I think a man would have to be inhumanly confident and self-reliant if he were to make this sort of voyage without faith in God."

Donald Crowhurst had no God. As all his friends would later attest, he was not a believer; and he thought those who were to be superstitious buffoons. Thus we now find him trapped on *Teignmouth Electron* with only his ego and his lies for company and comfort. And cold comfort they must have been. He was, perhaps, inhumanly confident – but only in his scheme, his dark truth.

Crowhurst did not know it, but at home things were not going well. Two days before Christmas, the Woodlands stable suffered a fire which destroyed the sails and rigging for Crowhurst's small sailboat *Pot of Gold*, and also did great damage to his workshop. Worse, Electron Utilisation's cash flow had not improved and, despite the emotional pressures and strained resources of the family related to Crowhurst's nautical enterprise, Best had begun to lobby for liquidation. Clare, busily trying to make the struggling company profitable, had little time for the children, who themselves felt under stress. Roger, for one, kept having nightmares about the ghostly apparition of his father staring silently at him from the door of his bedroom as he slept.

On the day after Christmas, Crowhurst discovered and closely examined split skin in the starboard float. This was no small matter, but rather a quite large split halfway along the float – not only allowing seepage, but also threatening the integrity of the deck attachments for the masthead shrouds. This was a repair that could not be made without supplies found only on land. Following this discovery, he zig-zagged in his course according to the prevailing winds, going any direction which kept the starboard float high against the waterline.

He'd by now crossed the Equator and was into the South-East Trades. Some 20 miles off the coast of Brazil and a thousand miles north of Rio, he worked at his fraudulent navigational log while circling endlessly outside shipping lanes, burning time. As part of this, he religiously logged radio traffic related to shipping routes and weather reports worldwide – noting facts which he would need in the fictional narrative of his fake voyage.

By the end of the first week of January Crowhurst had people at home believing he was beyond Tristan da Cunha and nearing the Cape of Good Hope – leaving them quite hopeful about their hero's prospects. Hallworth cabled him:

ROBIN LEADS   BERNARD BEYOND TASMANIA
TETLEY EASTERN INDIAN   YOUR AVERAGE
DAILY 30 MILES HIGHER   SUNDAY TIMES
RECKONS WINNER HOME APRIL NINE   THIS
YOUR TARGET

Two weeks later, before beginning eleven weeks of self-imposed radio-silence, Crowhurst sent two more cables – one to Hallworth, one to Best. To Hallworth he signaled the likelihood of upcoming radio silence due to mechanical problems – primarily the hatch leak which he (quite honestly) said continued to afflict the generator, and in turn power to his Marconi. He also indicated that coastal telegraph operators should until further notice listen for him between longitudes 80° east (roughly the center of the Indian Ocean) and 140° west (half-way between Cape Horn and New Zealand). This is where he supposedly would be within the next several weeks. He knew full well that if operators looked for him in those coordinates they would not find him. Thus the certainty of his upcoming radio-silence, no matter what the state of the generator. If he could not be found within the coordinates of where he was supposed to be, then it was safest not to be found anywhere.

He also cabled Stanley Best. To Best he wrote the following, exaggerating the poor condition of the vessel, and asking for a vital concession:

REGRET FLOAT FRAME SMASHED   SKIN SPLIT
DECK JOINTS PARTING   REPAIRS   NOT

HOLDING SPEED SO HORN AUTUMN   ILLFOUND
BOAT STOP   IF PREPARED DELETE CLAUSE
UNCONDITIONAL PURCHASE WILL TRY
OTHERWISE SUGGEST REVIEW NEWSPAPER
OFFERS   SOME DAYS IN HAND

Best, believing that Crowhurst was making a noble and honest effort, and that his life might be at risk if he pushed too fast, messaged back:

CABLE RECEIVED   DECISION YOURS STOP   NO
UNCONDITIONAL PURCHASE REQUIRED   GOOD
LUCK

At the same time, however, Best continued to press Clare for liquidation of the firm.

One wonders why Crowhurst even bothered, at this point, to ask for Best's blessing. Despite Best's willingness, Crowhurst must by now have realized he was so far – some 4,000 miles – from his publicly stated position, that he simply could not with honor retire into the nearest port. That would have given away his entire subterfuge.

Experienced navigators continued to view Crowhurst's claims with skepticism. In a summation of the race-to-date which he published in the *Sunday Times* on 2nd February, Francis Chichester commented:

> *Donald Crowhurst ... has claimed some fast bursts of speed, including a world record for the fastest day's run; but his average speed has not been fast – 101 miles per day – and*

at his last fix south of the Cape on January 10 he was about 8,800 miles behind Moitessier, so he does not seem a likely prize winner. ... Recently there have been a number of loose claims for distances and speeds sailed, and I hope that a sporting club will check and recognize speed claims as the Royal Aero Club and the Federation Aeronautique Internationale have done for flying.

No wiser words.

For the next few weeks – through all of February – Crowhurst would for the most part drift in silence through easy waters, staying as close to the South American coast as possible without detection. At the same time, he worked on his fake records and considered exactly where he might put-in to do the necessary repairs on the starboard float.

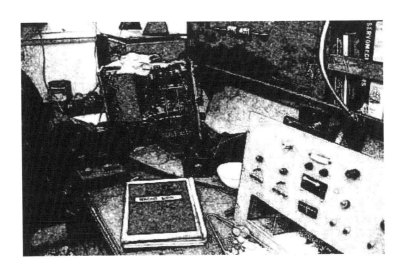

Chapter Fourteen: Rio Salado

It must have infuriated Crowhurst – perhaps at others, perhaps at himself – to realize he'd set out devoid of the spare plywood and rich mix of tools, screws, and other hardware and chandlery with which any vessel bound for such an extensive voyage should have been equipped. Indeed, such a collection had been assembled for Crowhurst, but had been left behind on the dock due to the chaos surrounding his final days before departure. Had he been equipped with such resources, he could have easily mended the split sheathing of the starboard hull, which was by now – early March – letting in more and more water, despite Crowhurst's leisurely loops at 20 to 30 miles per day, and his steadfastly avoiding high seas as much as possible. The only things he had in good supply were the circuits and fuses and wires meant for his much-advertised but still completely unbuilt computer.

He had to head in. There was no choice. But he consciously chose as inconspicuous and lonely an outpost as he could find, eventually settling on an isolated spot at the very top of Argentina's large Bahia Samorombón, near the mouth of the Rio de la Plata. At Rio Salado, Crowhurst's Pilot book promised a small settlement – but one large enough that Crowhurst would be able to find the necessary supplies. The place was described as simply a few sheds and a dirt road, with the most substantial presence being a three-man squad from Prefectura Nacional Marítima – the Argentinian Coast Guard. And even they did not have a telephone.

Thus Crowhurst dropped anchor near the tiny port on 6th March, at high tide. Using his usual prowess, Crowhurst managed to anchor on a sandbar even though his vessel was surrounded by deeper water. Once the tide ebbed, Crowhurst found himself aground.

The local Prefectura Nacional Marítima installation was such a small operation that the three-man staff did not even possess a boat. Senior Petty Officer Santiago Franchessi and one of his underlings hitched a ride out to Crowhurst with a local fisherman. Crowhurst had no Spanish, and the three locals no English. Crowhurst – dressed in a red shirt and khaki shorts – pointed to the damaged hull, and Franchessi did the math. The local boat pulled Crowhurst off the sandbar and then towed him to the empty Prefectura Nacional Marítima dock.

There was little to no efficient communication until Officer Franchessi recruited a French restaurant owner from 17 miles away to turn Crowhurst's rudimentary French into Spanish for Crowhurst's hosts. Crowhurst told them honestly that he was in a round-the-world "regatta." He told them dishonestly that he had just rounded Cape Horn, and was sure to emerge victorious in the regatta if he could only get the hull tended to. The Frenchman, Hector Salvati, later told journalists that Crowhurst seemed downright unbalanced: wracked with vast, quick mood-shifts – repeatedly swinging from tense darkness to giddy hilarity and then back again.

The next day, 8th March, Crowhurst undertook the repairs with supplies given him by Franchessi. That night, he dined with Franchessi and one other coast guarder. They served him up a steak, which Crowhurst clearly delighted in. Then, early on the morning of the 9th, Crowhurst got a tow back out to sea, and proceeded away.

Even though his final destination of home lay some 7,500 miles to the north-northeast, Crowhurst nevertheless sailed south. Simply stated: He needed to spend several weeks without a great deal of northward progress in order for his fake route to catch up with his actual position. (He planned 15th April as the date for making his fictional rounding of Cape Horn. This left him some six weeks in which to effectively be nowhere.) By heading south, he also opened himself to receiving weather reports out of Wellington, New Zealand, which info he needed for his fake log, still in progress.

Unknown to Crowhurst – or to anyone else in the world for another ten days or so – Moitessier had by this point, after taking on and defeating all three capes, decided to effectively take himself out of the race by continuing around the world again rather than making for England. At the time he rounded the Horn, Moitessier was more than well-positioned to win both awards. But the anti-materialist Moitessier had never cared much about the race, about "winning" in general, or about cash or fame. "My intention," he wrote the editors of the *Sunday Times* after he surprised everyone and arrived at Cape Town for the second time two and a half weeks into March, "is to continue the voyage, still nonstop, toward the Pacific Islands, where there is plenty of sun and more peace than in Europe. Please do not think I am trying to break a record. 'Record' is a very stupid word at sea. I am continuing nonstop because I am happy at sea, and perhaps because I want to save my soul."

That same day, the 18th, saw Nigel Tetley round Cape Horn in his battered and bruised trimaran.

The seas had not been kind to Tetley. At the end of February a rogue wave picked his boat up and, at high speed, tossed her forward to its crest. The steering cables – already repaired once by Tetley came apart while the boat slewed sideways in front of the breaking crest. The wave lifted the hull up so high that it seemed for a moment as if his vessel was on the verge of a cartwheel before the rogue dissolved into the sea from which it had emerged, and the trimaran regained balance.

A week later, Tetley was below decks when – during a gale – a second rogue hit, shattering a 6-foot-wide window of the saloon and completely blowing away the canvas curtain of the wheelhouse's starboard side. It seemed to Tetley as if half the frigid, 52° F sea now flooded the wheelhouse and flowed into the cabin like a waterfall through the cockpit doors. The event left everything – including Tetley – completely saturated, while the gale now blew a 48° F wind through the shattered window. For Tetley – with not even dry, warm clothes to change into – there was now virtually no difference between conditions below decks vs. those above decks. No shelter from the storm.

Floating debris in the cabin clogged the bilge-pump. Tetley bailed manually as best he could, and hastily "repaired" the lost window with a plank of plywood. He spent the rest of the night shivering in a damp sleeping bag, praying that another great wave would not come and do even more damage. Upon close inspection in the morning, he found broken frames and a sprung deck in the starboard hull. The main hull showed signs of coming apart – flexing with the whims of the ocean, throwing off splinters. In very sad shape overall. Nevertheless, on 18th March, he became the first multihull ever to make it round Cape Horn – and he pondered whether, with this accomplishment under his belt, he should retire. At the very least, his experience had confirmed for him what others had feared: a standard trimaran was by no means ideal for the Southern Ocean. Not at all. He considered himself lucky to be alive and wondered how Crowhurst might be faring.

Tetley's decision was made for him a week later when, during radio contact with the *Sunday Times*, he learned of Moitessier's abdication. This left Tetley in a position to achieve one of the prizes, possibly both. No one knew the status of the silent Crowhurst, who had last been heard from when supposedly in the Indian Ocean. Robin Knox-Johnston remained a similar mystery – having been silent since before Thanksgiving (due, though no-one but Knox-Johnston knew it, to loss of use of his transmitter).

In truth, at that moment, a massive NATO air- and sea-search was underway for Knox-Johnston whom many feared lost at sea in the mid-Atlantic near the Azores. In fact Knox-Johnston and his craft (also damaged and bandaged more than once) were pushing along quite well, but about a thousand miles to the southwest from where the searchers searched. Not until 6th April, when Knox-Johnston encountered a British tanker and communicated with her via Aldis lamp, were the skipper and his *Suhaili* back on the map. Word flashed back to Britain that he was alive, well, and anticipated finishing at Falmouth in two weeks time: thus making him the certain winner of the Golden Globe for being first solo sailor to successfully circumnavigate. The lapsed-time race looked like it would belong to Tetley, depending on the location and recent speeds of the mysterious Crowhurst.

Chapter Fifteen: The Noose of Laurels

At some point our deceits combine to form a cage. And this is what happened to Donald Crowhurst.

Crowhurst emerged from radio-silence on 10th April with a cable to Hallworth.

> DEVON NEWS EXETER – HEADING DIGGER
> RAMREZ LOG KAPUT 17697 28th WHAT'S NEW
> OCEANBASHING WISE

After so long a time of not hearing from their hero, there was relief and joy all around at receiving word from Crowhurst – most of all within the confines of Woodlands: "We were at home," remembers Simon Crowhurst, "and my mother told us, 'We've heard from your dad and he's done really well and he's on the way back.' She was just all smiles. In fact it's probably the last time I can remember ever seeing her completely happy. She was beaming. Just beaming."

Hallworth translated the language of the cable to mean that Crowhurst was nearing the Diego Ramirez Islands, some 60 miles west-southwest of Cape Horn, and that his logline had broken at 17697 miles – a handy idea of Crowhurst's, in case anyone back home wanted to take a look at it and found it considerably short of the mileage expected in a true round-the-world voyage. Three days after Hallworth's receipt of the cable, newspapers throughout Britain reported Crowhurst had rounded Cape Horn (a reasonable assumption based on Crowhurst's report of position on the 10th). The *Sunday Times* also estimated, given Crowhurst's implied daily rate of speed – 140 miles every 24 hours, which Chichester and others continued to find unlikely – that he'd put in at Teignmouth at the end of June or at latest the first week of July, the latter giving him a total voyage of approximately 250 days. As Hallworth duly informed Crowhurst, estimates for Tetley put him at 260 days. Thus Crowhurst was now ostensibly in line for the second (and more lucrative) prize.

In fact Crowhurst was northeast of Port Stanley – capital of the Falkland Islands. He'd tried transmitting in Morse on the frequency servicing Wellington Radio, New Zealand (the likely frequency for his fraudulent position) but had no success. Anxious to get reassuring word to Hallworth – and especially Clare – he compromised and eventually broadcast his "Digger Ramrez" cable via Radio General Pacheco, Buenos Aries, hoping no-one would notice he was supposedly at that moment still in the Southern Pacific, with the Andes standing between him and where his message was received. No-one did.

Crowhurst's fraudulent position merged with his actual position round about 16th April, at which point he – *at first* – began serious sailing towards home, hoping to win the cash and publicity he needed so desperately. Meanwhile Tetley, advised of his and Crowhurst's relative places in the races, did what he would not normally have done otherwise. He pushed his tattered vessel harder than he'd ever done before at a moment when she was weaker than she'd ever been before.

It was a foolish choice.

Tetley had done makeshift repairs to shore up a vessel that was, for all practical purposes, simply coming apart. A large section of the decking on the port and main hulls was about to fly away; and the beams beneath the vital cross-arm structure seemed ready to break at any moment. Add to this the fact that the port hull bow had been holed in several places. Water filled the hull. Tetley patched the largest hole in the port hull with plywood, and strengthened the cross-arm with roughly constructed but robust new beams. On this flimsy basis, he decided to continue on, racing for home, hoping for the lapsed-time prize. Had he known Crowhurst's true story, he could have taken his time, chosen his weather, and perhaps made it back safely. But he believed, wrongly, that he was in the midst of an honorable and honest race, and proceeded accordingly.

Knox-Johnston arrived at Falmouth on 22nd April, winning the Golden Globe. His voyage had taken him 312 days, with an average of 96.5 miles per day. Nearly a month later, on 21st May, Tetley's weary vessel gave way and sank a mere 1,200 miles away from home, in a storm off the Azores. Tetley managed to get off a Mayday message with coordinates, and pushed away in his little inflatable life raft in time to watch *Victress* – which he'd always referred to lovingly as *Vicky* – sink beneath the waves. He was shortly rescued.

Crowhurst received word of Tetley's disaster on the 23rd and fired off a cable:

> EVELYN TETLEY – SYMPATHISE DAVY JONES DIRTY TRICK   REJOICE MASTER SALVAGED – CROWHURST

Ironically, in inspiring Tetley's aggressive sailing by his lies, Crowhurst had not only destroyed Tetley's boat and Tetley's hope for the prize, but also his own last chance of getting out of his situation with some shred of dignity.

His stated speeds had dramatically decreased over the previous week, or so – coming to approximate his real speeds, which slowed as well. Given weather conditions for his coordinates, he could have made better time, but consciously did not. Why?

It is likely Crowhurst had come to ponder whether his fake logbooks would withstand inspection from experts, and whether or not he would actually get away with his fraud. For all his magical thinking, Crowhurst was nevertheless no idiot.

He must have realised, when brought face to face with the matter, that knowledgeable analysts would surely detect irregularities in even his most carefully calculated fake sun sights and other navigational and weather notes. He'd not be able to survive such scrutiny. Thus it is likely that sometime in early May he made a conscious decision to come in second, rather than first, in the lapsed-time race. He'd still be one of only three starters to have finished, and would thus still gain some share or notoriety and a great deal of respect – perhaps enough even to somehow salvage his floundering business and appease Best. At the same time, however, a second-place lapsed-time showing would not in turn require the type of close examination of his records which would inevitably be the fate of a winner. But with Tetley's loss, Crowhurst's "victory" in the lapsed-time race became inevitable, as did the scrutiny which would come with it. A noose of laurels.

Crowhurst was right to be wary. Chichester was by this time quite loud, albeit behind closed doors, about his suspicions of fraud on the part of Crowhurst. To Robert Riddell, race secretary for the *Sunday Times*, he wrote:

> *Dear Robert,*
> *First re D.C.: we don't want to hold up his reward a second longer than necessary. Can you do the following (if you agree about it)?*
> *Prepare a list of his authenticated messages and positive position statements, with, of course, dates. Particularly we should consider as soon as possible, his last message on leaving the S. Atlantic for the Southern Ocean, his first message, position, etc. on nearing the Horn .... . We need to*

know why the silence from Cape to the Horn (from an electronics engineer too) ... . Why did he never give exact positions? It also appeared that he had an extraordinary increase of speed on entering the S. Ocean; I think he claimed 13,000 miles in 10 weeks, or something, which seems most peculiar considering his slow speed for the previous long passage to the Cape ... . If you would let me have this information as soon as possible it may well save embarrassment later ... .

Sincerely,
Francis

Crowhurst doddled and delayed the inevitable triumph. For the two weeks after Tetley's collapse he sailed along coastal north-eastern Brazil, returning to the tropics. Breezes were light; seas low. He let the vessel tend herself, often on just the jib and mizzen. Early June found him back again across the Equator, steering slowly towards the Horse Latitudes and the weeds and other floating randomness of the strange Sargasso Sea. He worked at repairing his Marconi Kestrel, which had broken down after the failure of its power convertor, and eventually got it working. He also made more boisterous, brave tape recordings posing as the great circumnavigator he was not – just another self-effacing British hero: another Hillary, another Knox-Johnston.

He received a telegram from the BBC on 18th June which must have made his situation much less abstract:

CONGRATULATIONS ON PROGRESS   HAVE
NETWORK TELEVISION PROGRAMME FOR DAY

OF RETURN   YOUR FILM URGENTLY WANTED
CAN YOU PREPARE FILM AND TAPES
INFORMATION   ANY SUGGESTIONS PLEASE ON
GETTING IT BACK AT LEAST FOUR DAYS BEFORE
TEIGNMOUTH ARRIVAL   CAN ARRANGE BOAT
OR HELICOPTER HOW CLOSE AZORES BRITTANY
OFF SCILLES   REPLY URGENTLY = DONALD
KERR

Five days later, according to his logs, Crowhurst evidently stopped making any attempt to sail his vessel in any direction whatsoever. He and his boat drifted aimlessly upon one of the most silent and hallucinatory spots in all the oceans of the world. Though ominous in its own way, the Sargasso Sea was everything the Roaring Forties were not: sleepy, sullen, other-worldly – bounded to the west by the Gulf Stream, to the north by the North Atlantic Current, to the east by the Canary Current, and to the south by the North Atlantic Equitorial Current – all of these currents depositing their flotsam and jetsam into its hushed, spooky, sea-weed covered waters. A desert in the middle of the Atlantic. Here, in this most lonely and distant of places, Crowhurst left reality – and all the cares of the world – behind forever, descending into madness.

From here on in, Crowhurst's logs consisted of nothing but the details of a great revelation with which he'd been blessed: a previously unimagined Truth which now revealed itself to him alone, of all the populations of the world through time immemorial. For some 25,000 words he went on about the bulk of the human race being afflicted with "stalled minds" while a few truly great thinkers – he among them – were capable of massive intuitive leaps in philosophy, with minds so advanced they could even slip the bounds of the body and escape the flesh into an "extra physical" existence: an existence made possible by what he called "creative abstraction." With the force of his mental capacity and will, he could leave his body behind and ascend into a heightened reality of natural truth and beauty: the pure mathematics and physics of the cosmos. Coincidentally, of course, he could also escape his more-prosaic predicament in the real world, which became more and more real with every incoming cable, such as this one of 28th June from Hallworth:

> BBC AND EXPRESS MEETING YOU WITH CLARE
> AND ME OFF SCILLES · YOUR TRIUMPHS
> BRINGING ONE HUNDRED THOUSAND FOLK
> TEIGNMOUTH WHERE FUND NOW REACHING
> FIFTEEN HUNDRED PLUS OTHER BENEFITS
> PLEASE GIVE ME SECRETS OF TRIP NEAR DEATH
> AND ALL THAT FOR PRE-PRESS SELLING
> OPPORTUNITIES   MONEY OUTLOOK GOOD
> REPLY URGENT   THINKING ABOUT
> ADVERTISING

Hallworth would later speculate that he might actually have killed Crowhurst with this cable. Crowhurst's continued ravings in his logs ended finally on 1st July, three days after Hallworth's message, at which point it appears he "left his body" of his own free and manifest will, slipping over the side of his vessel at 11:20 AM plus 40 seconds – a moment in time which apparently, for him, carried some mystical meaning – consigning his flesh, though not his out of body intellect, to the deep. Thus he found escape not only from physical existence, but from all worldly troubles.

Nine days later, the captain and crew of the Royal Mail Vessel *Picardy* stumbled upon *Teignmouth Electron* ghosting along on her mizzen. *Picardy* was travelling from London to the Caribbean. Her path crossed with that of the trimaran at Latitude 33° 11' North, Longitude 40° 28' West. This is almost dead center of the Atlantic, and roughly 1,800 miles from England, 600 miles southwest of the Azores. Finding no-one aboard, the crew hoisted the trimaran up onto the deck of the *Picardy*, notified the proper authorities, and began a search of the immediate waters, hoping against hope to find Crowhurst, whom it was at first assumed had fallen overboard.

Herald Express reporter John Ware was among the first to hear the news back home. "Thousands of wellwishers were expected to flock in to cheer the master mariner, and a flotilla of boats would accompany the trimaran as it crossed the finishing line, with Crowhurst towed into the harbour to face the world's press and film cameras. So that phone call was a stunner. I immediately contacted the man who was masterminding the victory parade ... Rodney Hallworth. He hadn't heard the news. It took a lot to keep 'Rodders' quiet, but for once he was lost for words. 'It can't be; I don't believe it,' was his first reaction."

On 13th July, all of Britain awoke to word of Crowhurst's loss. Chichester, setting his suspicions aside, commented: "It is very sad that such an extraordinary accident should have occurred to such a gallant sailor after such a memorable voyage and so near home. But before he was lost, he had accomplished something near to his heart, having circumnavigated the world." Knox-Johnston, now the defacto winner of the lapsed-time race as well as the Golden Globe, announced he'd be donating his £5000 prize to the Donald Crowhurst Appeal Fund launched by the *Sunday Times* with the mission of helping support Crowhurst's widow and children. The newspaper matched that amount. The BBC promised to pay into the fund the fees it would have otherwise paid Crowhurst for his films. Stanley Best – lest he look like Ebenezer Scrooge – quite publicly waived his claims on Crowhurst's property. And the Royal Mail pledged to return the trimaran to Britain at its own expense – although this never occurred. (The vessel wound up being sold, repaired, and used for several years to entertain tourists on Montego Bay in Jamaica before being acquired by a new owner and being damaged in a hurricane near Cayman Brac, where she has lain ashore, slowly disintegrating, ever since.)

Thankfully, great sympathy for the family was in no way dulled or minimized when, on 27th July, after close examination of Crowhurst's logbooks, news of his deception blared out even more loudly than had news of his loss.

Chapter Sixteen: Echoes

One of the last owners of *Teignmouth Electron* before her abandonment said he believed she was haunted. When trying to sleep below in the cabin, he routinely heard footsteps moving across the unpopulated deck.

Three years after the race, on 5th February 1972, Nigel Tetley was found a suicide, hanging from a tree in some woods near Dover. Although he'd not made it back to his home port in 1969, he'd succeeded in circumnavigating the globe by crossing his own outbound and inbound routes, becoming the first multihull soloist to do so. For this the *Sunday Times* awarded him a consolation prize of £1000, which he used to help fund the building of a new trimaran. Tetley moored *Miss Vicky* at Sandwich on the River Stour. As before, he and his wife lived aboard. He wrote a book about his Golden Globe experience entitled *Trimaran Solo*. But he was not a gifted writer. Critics panned the prose as dull, and sales reflected the reviews. He sought sponsors for another round the world effort, but none came forward, and it always chagrined Tetley that the cheating Crowhurst continued, even in death, to garner more attention than himself.

Crowhurst and his misadventure have lived on in the arts. There's a critically-acclaimed 1982 French film – *Les Quarantièmes rugissants* (*The Roaring Forties*) – inspired by Crowhurst's story. Artist Tacita Dean has created two video pieces entitled *Disappearance at Sea*, and has also written a book concerning Crowhurst. The 1991 Edinburgh Fringe Festival hosted a one-man play entitled *Strange Voyage*. Chris Van Strander's play *Daniel Pelican* (1999) shifted the Crowhurst tale to the 1920s. Another play, Jonathan Rich's *The Lonely Sea* (later revised as *Single-Handed)* gained attention as runner-up in the 1979 *Sunday Times* International Student Playwright competition. In 1998 the opera *Ravenshead* brought Crowhurst's tale to yet another medium, this followed by Daniel Brian's play *Almost a Hero* (2004) and in 2015 the multimedia stage event "The Last Voyage of Donald Crowhurst" put on by Calgary's Ghost River Theatre.

In literature, Robert Stone's brilliant *Outerbridge Reach* (1993) takes its inspiration from Crowhurst, as does Isabelle Autissier's 2009 novel *Seule la mer s'en souviendra* (*Only the sea will remember*). Poet Donald Finkel used Crowhurst's tale as the basis for a book-length narrative poem: *The Wake of the Electron* (1987).

I heartily recommend the excellent Film Four document-ary *Deep Water* (2006), which includes a range of fascinating interviews with Crowhurst's surviving friends and family, as well as BBC footage including sections from Crowhurst's own reels shot aboard *Teignmouth Electron*. There is another film, *Crowhurst*, directed by Simon Rumley and released in 2015. As I write (July 2016), a full feature film starring Colin Firth as Crowhurst and Rachel Weisz as Clare is in post-production, scheduled for release in early 2017.

More importantly than haunting Teignmouth, or the arts, or what remains of his decimated boat, Crowhurst most profoundly haunts the family he left behind. "I used to dream about it for years," Clare told *The Guardian's* Robert McCrum in 2009, adding that she "used to be angry with Donald" as well as with herself. "It was a terrible thing to do to the children. … You know, I never thought he would raise the money. Then he was so full of excitement. Of course I wish I'd said, 'Don't go.' But at the time I thought he was doing the right thing – I was not being brave, but being loyal to his dream, as a wife. … I've lived on very little money these 40 years. I've muddled through. I still feel as if I'm muddling through. There are moments when I do feel extraordinarily happy, but then I feel guilty about it." She never remarried. "After it happened, I was just another mum, really. I was pursued for a while by one or two locals, but I really wasn't interested. Something died with Donald."

Speaking to the same journalist, son Simon commented: "I feel compelled to think about my father's story. … It's a story that people remember, and that's a consolation. It's a story that tells you something about what it means to be human." He keeps a small scale model of *Teignmouth Electron* in his office at Cambridge University. He's never travelled out to see the wreck, and mulls whether or not he should. His mother owns the actual logbooks and keeps them at her house, but Simon steers clear. "I'm wary of the logbooks. My wife doesn't like me thinking about them. They have a bad effect on me."

Simon's feelings about his father remain mixed. Once he'd grown to an age where he could understand the full story of his father's voyage, "I felt disappointment and shame, mixed with pride that he did do so much and that he struggled so hard. ... The worst thing about it is that he endangered Nigel Tetley, who pushed his boat beyond the limit when he was told of my father's 'position' and had to be rescued. That is reprehensible."

Simon insists however – and, I think, accurately – that his father set out with every intention of truly sailing round the world and achieving his goal with honesty and integrity, rather than with the initial intent to deceive. "Some people say that, but that's definitely not true. You can tell from the logbooks how bitterly, bitterly disappointed he was when he realised he wasn't going to be up to it. But the truth is, he broke just about every rule in the race. And he knew that. He did pay a terrible price for it. He wasn't happy about it – I'm sure of that. You can tell from his logbooks, he didn't revel in it. But you also realise that he did go really badly wrong, and that was down to him. You know, he decided to do that. Under duress, yes. But he got into that situation himself. No one else was to blame."

Remembering Knox-Johnston's kindness to his family – his gift of the £5000 prize – Simon notes: "It was such an incerdibly generous thing to do." Knox-Johnston has also been quite generous in his assessment of Crowhurst, which I will let be the last word here:

> ... there was ample time after leaving England and the din of the media to reflect on what lay ahead. I remember it well. Fear of the unknown is by far the greatest fear, and all the competitors had plenty to worry about. None of us knew whether a boat and a frail human were capable of sailing so long and so far, in such inhospitable waters. Would the boat stand up to it? Could a man endure a ten-month solitary confinement, with no one to see or talk to and no relief from hard labor and constant danger, without going mad? None of us knew. In the end, the race was the severest test I have ever faced, both physically and mentally ... .
>
> ... The factors of preparation, temperament, and circumstance loom huge at sea, and no-one should rush to criticize Donald Crowhurst. ... Let the ending not obscure the courage and resourcefulness of the man. He accomplished much in his final voyage, and his worst crime was falling short of his own vision.

Bibliography

A Race Too Far. Chris Eakin. Ebury Press, 2010.

A Voyage for Madmen. Peter Nichols. Profile Books, 2001.

A World of My Own. Robin Knox-Johnston. William Morrow, 1970.

Deep Water (Documentary Film). Pathé Pictures International, 2006.

"Deep Water." Robert McCrum. *The Guardian.* 4th April 2009.

"Donald Crowhurst and His Sea of Lies." David Jones. *The Daily Mail.* 4th November 2006.

"Donald Crowhurst's Son Tells His Story." Fiona Wingett. *London Sunday Times.* 3 February 2007.

"Drama on the Waves: The Life and Death of Donald Crowhurst." Ed Caeser. *The Independent* (UK). 27th October 2006.

"Funeral of Veteran Mariner." *Exeter Express & Echo* (UK). 11th March 2010.

"The Sins of the Father." Decca Aitkenhead. *The Guardian.* 27th October 2007.

The Strange Last Voyage of Donald Crowhurst. Nicholas Tomalin and Rob Hall. Hoddard & Stoughton, 1970.

Trimaran Solo. Nigel Tetley. Nautical Publishing Company, 1970.

About the Author

Edward Renehan has written more than 20 books for such houses as Doubleday, Oxford University Press, Crown, and Basic. At the same time he has pursued a lengthy career as an executive in the publishing field, having held positions at St. Martin's Press, Wiley, and other firms, including seven years as Director of Computer Publishing Programs for Macmillan. He currently serves as Managing Director of New Street Communications, LLC, the publisher of this book, and its sister firm New Street Nautical Audio. Renehan and his wife live in Wickford, Rhode Island – just outside Newport. He is an avid blue water sailor.

Also of Interest ...

CAPSIZED

Jim Nalepka's Epic 119 Day Survival Voyage Aboard the Rose-Noëlle

By *New York Times* Bestselling Author

STEVEN CALLAHAN, author of *Adrift*

Available in Kindle, Paper, and Audio Editions

KIRKUS: Soulful, emotional ... earnest and engrossing.

Adam Braver: While the suspense, drama, and harrowing adventure of *Capsized* will no doubt grip any reader, it shouldn't be missed that Steve Callahan's book also is about the complexity of the individual and the collective. Callahan shows us disparate people forced to rely upon each other for their mutual survival.

Publishers Weekly: An intriguing tale of personal victories claimed from disaster.

Herb McCormick: One of the classic sea stories of this or any other era. ... A psychological thriller, a seafaring mystery, and of course a saga of adventure.

newstreetcommunications.com

newstreetnautical.com

64135140R00067

Made in the USA
Charleston, SC
21 November 2016